DR. WISDOM FOR PRESIDENT: BEYOND WISDOM

Leading with wisdom beyond politics

Dr. Wisdom Zerit Teklay

Wisdom People Party

Copyright © 2023 DR. WISDOM ZERIT TEKLAY

"Copyright © 2023 by Dr. Wisdom Zerit Teklay and the Wisdom People Party. All rights reserved. This publication, in any form—electronic, mechanical, photocopying, recording, or otherwise—cannot be reproduced or transmitted without Dr. Teklay's written permission. This includes all digital distribution and sharing.

Published in the United States, this work is Dr. Wisdom Zerit Teklay's intellectual property. It offers general information derived from his Natural Medicine Philosophy, providing insights for societal well-being. It is important to note that this book is not a medical guide. The content, reflecting Dr. Teklay's personal applications and philosophies, should not be construed as professional medical advice or treatment.

For permissions beyond private study, scholarship, or research, contact Dr. Teklay at zeritprrcw@gmail.com or call +1 615 970 1832. Unauthorized use may result in copyright infringement under U.S. law.

The author expressly disclaims liability and is not responsible for any consequences resulting from the application of information contained in this book. The information provided is intended for general understanding and does not replace professional medical advice."

"In the pursuit of wisdom, we transcend the boundaries of politics and find the seeds of change. Let us sow these seeds in the soil of unity and nurture them with the spirit of freedom, so they may grow into a forest of peace that shelters all humanity."

DR. WISDOM ZERIT TEKLAY

CONTENTS

Title Page

Copyright

Epigraph

Foreword

Introduction

Preface

Prologue

DR. WISDOM FOR PRESIDENT BEYOND WISDOM

Chapter 1 Visionary Eritrean-American Polymath Philopher   6
of Zerit-Tonianism Philosophy   Journey to

Chapter 2	14
Chapter 3	17
Chapter 4	18
Chapter 5	21
Chapter 6	24
Chapter 7	30
Chapter 8	36
Chapter 9	39
Chapter 10	44
Chapter 11	49
Chapter 12	52

Chapter 13	57
Chapter 14	60
Chapter 15	68
Chapter 16	71
Chapter 17	79
Chapter 18	86
Chapter 19	93
Chapter 20	107
Chapter 21	114
Chapter 22	122
Chapter 23	125
Chapter 24	127
Chapter 25	132
Chapter 26	138
Chapter 27	149
Chapter 28	162
Chapter 29	165
Chapter 30	173
Chapter 31	177
Chapter 32	189
Chapter 33	192
Chapter 34	197
Chapter 35	205
Chapter 36	211
Chapter 37	218
Chapter 38	221
Chapter 39	226
Chapter 40	229

Chapter 41	233
Chapter 43	241
Chapter 44	243
CHAPTER 45	246
Epilogue	250
Afterword	252
Acknowledgement	254
About The Author	256
Praise For Author	260
Books By This Author	262

FOREWORD

In a world often divided by partisan lines, where political discourse is marred by polarization and short-term gains overshadow long-term vision, "Dr. Wisdom for President: Beyond Wisdom - Leading with Wisdom Beyond Politics" emerges as a timely and necessary beacon of hope and guidance.

This book is more than just an exploration of political leadership; it is a profound journey into the essence of wisdom in guiding societies towards a harmonious and prosperous future. At a time when the clamor of politics often drowns out the voice of reason and humanity, the author invites us to pause and reflect on what it truly means to lead with wisdom.

The pages of this book are filled with insights that challenge conventional political thought and practice. It dares to ask questions that many shy away from. What does it mean to lead beyond the typical scope of politics? How can wisdom transform not only the way we govern but also how we perceive leadership in its entirety?

Through a blend of philosophical musings, practical insights, and lessons drawn from both history and contemporary times, this book offers a fresh perspective on political leadership. It is a call to current and future leaders, and indeed to all of us, to rethink the role of wisdom in shaping our world. The author skillfully navigates through complex ideas, presenting them in a manner that is both engaging and enlightening.

"DFR Wisdom for President: Beyond Wisdom - Leading with Wisdom Beyond Politics" is not just a book for politicians or those interested in governance; it is a book for anyone who believes in the power of wise leadership to create a better world. It is an invitation to embark on a journey of discovery, one that explores the depths of wisdom and its potential to revolutionize our approach to leadership and governance.

As you delve into this book, prepare to be challenged, inspired, and transformed. The journey you are about to embark on is not just about understanding leadership in a new light; it is about envisioning a future where wisdom guides our decisions, policies, and actions. This is a book for our times, a guiding light in an often tumultuous world, offering a path to a more wise and enlightened form of leadership

INTRODUCTION

In an era where political landscapes are perpetually turbulent, and leadership is often questioned, "Dr. Wisdom for President: Beyond Wisdom - Leading with Wisdom Beyond Politics" emerges as a beacon of insight and guidance. This book is not merely about the practical aspects of political leadership; it delves deeper into the philosophical and ethical dimensions that are often overlooked yet are crucial for transformative governance.

At its core, this manuscript challenges conventional political wisdom, advocating for a leadership style that transcends traditional political boundaries and ideologies. It's a call for a new kind of leader - one who leads with wisdom, integrity, and a deep understanding of the human condition. This book is for those who aspire to make a genuine difference in the world of politics, not by wielding power but by embodying wisdom and compassion in their leadership approach.

Through a blend of theoretical discourse, practical insights, and real-world examples, "Dr. Wisdom for President" invites readers to rethink what it means to lead. It's an exploration of how wisdom can be the guiding force in political leadership, influencing policies and decisions that are not only effective but also morally sound and socially responsible.

As we navigate through these pages, we embark on a journey beyond the surface-level tactics of politics. We delve into the essence of true leadership - one that is rooted in wisdom, driven by a vision for the greater good, and unshaken by the transient trends of political theatrics. This book is a testament to the belief that the future of effective governance lies in leading with wisdom beyond politics.

PREFACE

In an age where the cacophony of political discourse often drowns out the voice of wisdom, this book seeks to offer a beacon of clarity and insight. "Dr. Wisdom for President Beyond Wisdom: Leading with Wisdom Beyond Politics" is more than just a collection of thoughts; it is an odyssey through the realms of wisdom, leadership, and the transformative power of visionary ideas.

My journey, both personal and political, has been deeply influenced by the enduring love and guidance of my parents, Teklay Sebhatleab and Tiebe Mebrahtu, and the unwavering support of my family and friends. Their influence is a golden thread woven throughout this narrative. This book is also a tribute to the valiant heroes of Eritrean and American freedom, whose sacrifices have illuminated the path of liberty and justice.

At the heart of this work lies my dream for a United States of America â€" a dream of unity under one constitution, one currency, and one flag, symbolizing the unbreakable spirit of a continent. This vision is dedicated to the gallant freedom fighters who laid down their lives for the sovereignty of their nations and to the courageous souls who rose against the chains of slavery.

As the founder of Amazoxa Peace University and the pioneer of Zerit-Tonianism, my life's work has been dedicated to breaking barriers and building bridges. The Wisdom People Party, under my leadership, stands not just as a political entity but as a movement towards a future where wisdom supersedes politics, where leadership is not just about power but about empowering, and where peace and unity are not mere ideals but tangible realities.

This book is an invitation to explore the potential of wisdom-led leadership in transcending political divides and fostering a global ethos of understanding and cooperation. It is a call to each reader to be a part of this transformative journey, to challenge the status quo, and to embrace a future beyond the confines of conventional politics.

As you turn these pages, I invite you to journey with me through ideas and ideals, through challenges and solutions, and most importantly, through a vision of a world led not by mere politics, but by wisdom beyond politics.

PROLOGUE

In the quiet corridors of history, away from the tumultuous arenas of political power, there has always been a whisper, a subtle call for a different kind of leadership - one that is rooted not in the pursuit of power, but in the depth of wisdom. This book is born from that whisper, a response to the yearning for a leadership that transcends the usual bounds of politics and touches the realms of wisdom.

"Wisdom," as we often forget, is not just about knowledge or experience; it is about understanding the deeper currents of human nature, society, and the world at large. It is about seeing beyond the immediate, beyond the superficial allure of power and prestige. This book envisions a world where leaders are not just politicians, but sages; where the compass guiding decisions is not just political expediency, but profound wisdom.

As you turn these pages, you will embark on a journey back to the roots of true leadership. You will rediscover what it means to lead with a vision that is clear, not clouded by the narrow confines of partisan politics. You will meet figures from history and learn from their insights, seeing how their wisdom shaped not just their times, but the course of the future.

This is not just a book about political theory or leadership strategy. It is a call to awaken the sage within, to rise above the din of divisive politics, and to lead with a wisdom that is

word at a time.
God bless Zerit-Tonianism, God bless Amazoxa Peace University, and God bless the world we are yet to build together.
Thank you.

as timeless as it is necessary in our times. It is a call to every aspiring leader, every citizen, and every person who believes that the heart of true leadership is not power, but wisdom.

In a world teeming with challenges and at the brink of pivotal changes, "Dr. Wisdom for President: Beyond Wisdom - Leading with Wisdom Beyond Politics" is more than just a book. It is a manifesto, a guide, and a beacon of hope for a new era of leadership — an era that values wisdom above all.

DR. WISDOM FOR PRESIDENT BEYOND WISDOM

DR. WISDOM ZERIT TEKLAY

Dr. Wisdom for President: beyond wisdom-
Leading with Wisdom: Beyond Politics

DEDICATION

"I dedicate this work to my parents, Teklay Sebhatleab and Tiebe Mebrahtu, for their love and guidance; to my family and friends, for their unwavering support; and to the heroes of Eritrean and American freedom. This book also honors my dream of the United States of Africa - united under one constitution, one currency, and one flag. It is a tribute to all freedom fighters who sacrificed their lives for the independence and autonomy of their nations, and to those brave souls who fought tirelessly to abolish slavery. This work celebrates my legacies: initiating a non-violent revolution to abolish the U.S. natural-born citizen requirement for presidential eligibility, leading the Wisdom People Party, founding Amazoxa Peace University, and pioneering Zerit-Tonianism. May it inspire future generations in their pursuit of liberty, unity, and a harmonious Africa."

Introduction

Dr.Wisdom for President: Beyond Wisdom Leading with Wisdom Beyond Politics" is an enlightening book that delves into the extraordinary life and philosophy of Dr. Wisdom Zerit Teklay, an Eritrean-American polymath, philosopher, and natural medicine nutritionist. This compelling narrative showcases Dr. Teklay's visionary leadership and his establishment of Amazoxa Peace University, a symbol of his dedication to global harmony and personal empowerment.

Through the pages, readers embark on a transformative journey exploring Zerit-Tonianism, Dr. Teklay's unique philosophical framework that emphasizes wisdom, justice, and human dignity. The book illustrates how his philosophy transcends the material realm, advocating for the power of knowledge to uplift humanity. Dr. Teklay's holistic approach, which integrates the mind, body, and spirit, is a testament to his commitment to comprehensive well-being.

This book is not just about a presidential candidacy; it's a reflection of Dr. Teklay's embodiment of wisdom and exceptional leadership. His insights, available on his Amazon Author Page and through his writings, invite readers into a world of intellectual adventure, promoting cultural harmony and advocating for justice and equality.

"Dr Wisdom for President: beyond wisdom-leading with wisdom beyond politics" is more than a biography; it's a call to action for a more inclusive and equal future. It supports the petition advocating for the amendment of the U.S. Constitution to abolish the natural-born citizen requirement, championing merit over birthplace in leadership. This book is a beacon of hope and inspiration, urging readers to join a movement that redefines the essence of knowledge and leadership in the modern world.

CHAPTER 1
VISIONARY ERITREAN-AMERICAN POLYMATH PHILOPHER OF ZERIT-TONIANISM PHILOSOPHY JOURNEY TO JUSTICE

A Vision for a Unified World: The Legacy of Dr. Wisdom Zerit Teklay

As Dr. Wisdom Zerit Teklay, my attributes position me as an effective and successful officeholder. My intellectual depth and visionary leadership are demonstrated through my initiative, self-reliance, and commitment to education, notably as the founder and inaugural graduate of Amazoxa Peace University. My multiple doctorate degrees in various fields showcase my broad expertise, particularly in governance. These degrees, uniquely obtained from Amazoxa Peace University, an institution I established, underscore my dedication to personal educational philosophies and innovative learning. I taught myself at this institution, becoming its first self-graduate, with a self-administered accreditation process for my doctorates. This unconventional academic journey highlights my commitment to innovative education.

My books, "Wisdom 101" and "Dr. Wisdom for President," disseminate wisdom and inspire change. I have also founded initiatives like the "Modern Birth Certificate" and "World Independence Day," reflecting my innovative thinking and dedication to social justice and inclusivity.

My philosophy, "Wisdom 101," positions wisdom as the cornerstone of leadership, exemplifying my ethical compass and dedication to wise decision-making. As a natural healer and educator at Amazoxa Peace University, I empower others, creating a ripple effect of inspiration for a better future. My principle of "the people, by the people, for the people," underscores my dedication to public service, and I embody the principles of Zerit-Tonianism, promoting justice, equality, and human dignity.

Additionally, as an Inspirational Organic Comedian, I employ humor for positive change and engaging communication. My global perspective fosters understanding and unity across cultures. My intellectual depth, visionary leadership, and commitment to positive change suggest my potential as a successful, impactful officeholder.

My ultimate legacy would be the realization of a unified world, where wisdom guides leadership, transcending national borders for collective problem-solving, and prioritizing well-being, peace, cooperation, and sustainable development. I envision a future with equitable resource management, conflict resolution through diplomacy, global knowledge sharing, and a unified flag and constitution symbolizing our shared humanity.

This legacy aims for a world transformed by wisdom, united in purpose, thriving in harmony. Through my work, leadership, and commitment to global unity, I strive to make this vision a reality. Despite challenges, my optimism and determination are fueled by the belief that the human spirit, guided by wisdom and compassion, is key to a better future.

My legacy will be measured not by material possessions or accolades, but by the positive impact I have on the world, the lives I touch, the barriers I break down, and the hope I inspire for a brighter future. I aim to be remembered as a force for good, a champion of wisdom, and a catalyst for global unity.

Beyond Wisdom - Leading with Wisdom Beyond Politics

In support of my motion for summary judgment, I present my book, "Beyond Wisdom - Leading with

Wisdom Beyond Politics," as an integral part of my case documentation. This work offers valuable insights and perspectives that I am confident will guide the court's deliberations and contribute to reaching a just and equitable decision regarding my eligibility to run for president.

Thank you for your valuable time and thoughtful consideration.

Sincerely,

Dr. Wisdom Zerit Teklay

UNITED STATES DISTRICT COURT

FOR THE DISTRICT OF COLUMBIA

DR. WISDOM ZERIT TEKLAY,

Plaintiff,

v.

FEDERAL ELECTION COMMISSION,

Defendant.

MOTION FOR SUMMARY JUDGMENT

I. INTRODUCTION

II. STATEMENT OF UNDISPUTED MATERIAL FACTS

III. ARGUMENT

A. The "Natural Born Citizen" Clause is Unconstitutional as Applied to Dr. Teklay

B. Dr. Teklay is a "Natural Born Citizen" Within the Constitution's Meaning

IV. CONCLUSION

For these compelling reasons, Dr. Teklay respectfully urges the Court to enter summary judgment in his favor, courageously declaring the "natural born Citizen" clause unconstitutional when applied to him.

Respectfully submitted,

Dr. Wisdom Zerit Teklay

Plaintiff

Date: Wednesday, November 22, 2023

MOTION FOR SUMMARY JUDGMENT

Statement of Undisputed Material Facts

Argument

Conclusion

Based on these arguments, Plaintiff urgently requests the Court to grant this Motion for Summary Judgment and affirm his undeniable eligibility to serve as the President of the United States.

Dated: Wednesday, November 22, 2023

Respectfully submitted,

Dr. Wisdom Zerit Teklay

Plaintiff

Office Number: +1 615 970 1832

Email: zeritprrcw@gmail.com

Navigating the Labyrinth of Eligibility: Dr. Wisdom Zerit Teklay's Path to the Presidency

Dr. Teklay faces a significant hurdle in realizing his ambitions: the "natural born citizen" clause. Yet, he remains undeterred and resolute in his pursuit. Whether through seeking a constitutional amendment or challenging the interpretation through litigation, Dr. Teklay demonstrates his unwavering belief in serving the United States and his willingness to explore unconventional paths. His success would not only fulfill his personal aspirations but also set a historic precedent for future candidates, reinforcing the inclusivity and fairness of our democratic process.

A Legal Defense for Dr. Teklay's Presidential Aspirations

The "natural born citizen" clause, while open to legal debate, can be compellingly argued in favor of Dr. Teklay. By adopting a broader interpretation that considers historical records, the Fourteenth Amendment, and Supreme Court precedents, we can establish a strong legal foundation supporting Dr. Teklay's unequivocal eligibility for the presidency. This comprehensive and well-founded defense bolsters the credibility of Dr. Teklay's presidential aspirations.

Navigating Constitutional Barriers: Dr. Teklay's Pursuit of the American Presidency

Dr. Teklay's remarkable journey from foreign birth to U.S. citizenship is meticulously detailed in his writings. His challenge against the FEC to overturn the constitutional provision barring his presidency is based on a careful and thorough analysis of Article II, Section 1, Clause 5. By courageously contesting the status quo, Dr. Teklay calls for a just and equitable reinterpretation of the "natural born Citizen" clause. His pursuit goes beyond personal ambition, addressing critical questions of equitable representation and the true essence of American identity.

CHAPTER 2

EMBRACING A WORLD OF WISDOM, JUSTICE, AND EQUALITY: THE TRANSFORMING VISION OF AMAZOXA PEACE UNIVERSITY

Amazoxa Peace University (APU): A Beacon of Transformation Through Zerit-Tonianism

Amazoxa Peace University (APU) is a non-profit institution dedicated to transforming individuals and societies through the teachings of Zerit-Tonianism, a philosophy developed by Dr. Wisdom Zerit Teklay. This philosophy emphasizes the pursuit of wisdom, justice, equality, and holistic well-being. APU aims to address critical issues such as limited access to transformative education, societal injustices, and materialistic mindsets. The headquarters of APU will be located in the United States of America and Eritrea.

Mission Statement

APU is committed to empowering individuals and communities to cultivate wisdom, justice, equality, and holistic well-being through the transformative power of Zerit-Tonianism.

Problem Statement

The world faces pressing challenges that hinder personal and societal progress, including:

Solution

APU serves as a beacon of positive change by:

Long-Term Vision

APU envisions a world transformed by Zerit-Tonianism, characterized by:

Grant Proposal

APU seeks grant funding to support its mission of societal transformation through Zerit-Tonianism. The funds will be utilized to:

Impact

APU's impact will be evident in:

Conclusion

Amazoxa Peace University stands as a catalyst for positive transformation, empowering individuals and societies to embrace the principles of Zerit-Tonianism. With grant support, APU aims to cultivate wisdom, justice, equality, and holistic well-being, creating a brighter future for all.

CHAPTER 3

BEYOND BORDERS, BEYOND CONFLICT: A GLOBAL DREAM FOR PEACE AND UNITY

CHAPTER 4

FROM ZERIT TO WISDOM: A NAME CHANGE FOR A HIGHER PURPOSE

"Embracing Wisdom: A Journey to a Unified World" - A Compelling and Influential Author's Message

From Zerit to Wisdom: A Name Change for a Higher Purpose

I have changed my name from Zerit Teklay Sebhatleab to Wisdom Zerit Teklay. This is not a mere act of vanity, but a profound declaration of my unwavering commitment to a world united by wisdom, transcending borders. To me, wisdom is more than an intellectual pursuit. It is a shield against division, a bridge across cultures, and a weapon of understanding. Wisdom is the antidote to fear, the fuel for compassion, and the key to a future where "us" versus "them" dissolves into a collective "we."

My journey began with a profound realization: the wounds of our world stem from ignorance. Thus, I have chosen wisdom as my guiding light, my compass. It is not a destination, but a path that I invite you to walk alongside me. Together, we can be the catalyst for change. We are the healers, the reasoners, the unifiers. We are the architects of a world where peace is not just a prayer, but our shared purpose. This book serves as a testament to that belief. It is a battle cry against injustice, a blueprint for unity, and a reminder that no one is exempt from the law of love. It is a spark waiting to ignite the fire of change within each one of us. I am Wisdom, and I walk this path with many.

About the Author and His Enduring Dream

I, Wisdom Zerit Teklay, dream of a world united under one banner, one constitution, and one infinite sea of solutions. A world where the phrase "Dreams come true one day" is not just a slogan, but our daily mantra. While I may not witness this unity in my lifetime, I believe in the power of echoes. I trust that the ideas presented in this book will resonate through generations, creating a symphony of hope that brings us ever closer to that dream. Though my voice may not reach the United Nations, yours can. If I cannot be the global voice, let this book be your megaphone. Let its pages resound with your rallying cry, gathering the world under the banner of wisdom. This is not about me. This is about us. This is about humanity rising, hand in hand, to write a new chapter in our collective story.

Championing the Collective Dream

This book is not just a manifesto; it is a movement. A movement fueled by the collective dreams of every soul yearning for a better tomorrow. It is a call to action, urging us to bridge divides, replace suspicion with empathy, and trade weapons for words. The path ahead may be treacherous, but our unity is our strength. Let us walk it together, guided by the wisdom within each and every one of us. Let us build a world where every child sleeps under the same flag, the flag of unity, the flag of wisdom.

Join me in making history. Let us wield wisdom as our weapon, our shield, our song. Let us make the world resonate with its chorus. This is our story. This is wisdom.

CHAPTER 5

DR. WISDOM ZERIT TEKLAY: A HEALING PIONEER

Dr. Wisdom Zerit Teklay: A Q&A with a Doctor of Natural Medicine and Global Visionary

Unlock the Extraordinary: Discover the World of Dr. Wisdom Zerit Teklay, a Doctor of Natural Medicine Like No Other

Q: Dr. Wisdom Zerit Teklay, what compelled you to pursue natural medicine?
A: Since an early age, I have observed the limitations of conventional medicine, where people often long for solutions beyond pharmaceuticals. This observation led me to recognize the immense potential of natural healing and the profound ability of the human body to restore itself. This realization ignited my purpose, and I dedicated my life to exploring and

understanding these natural healing processes.

Q: And thus, Zerit-Tonian Nutrition was born?
A: Absolutely! Zerit-Tonian Nutrition transcends traditional dieting to become a guiding philosophy. We view food as medicine, tailoring its composition to address the unique needs and imbalances of each individual. By harnessing the power of herbs, whole foods, and natural rhythms, we empower the body to embark on a transformative journey of healing.

Q: You mentioned being more than just a doctor; could you elaborate?
A: Indeed. My approach to healing is holistic, recognizing that true well-being encompasses mind, body, and spirit. This understanding led me to develop Amazoxa-Nism, a philosophy that extends beyond conventional medicine to include peace, justice, equality, and global well-being. We believe that individual health is intrinsically linked with the welfare of the entire world.

Q: So, you're not just a doctor but also a philosopher and social leader?
A: Precisely. I see myself as a bridge builder, merging ancient wisdom with modern science, and linking personal healing with global transformation. This vision inspired me to establish Amazoxa Peace University (APU), where we educate and empower others to join this remarkable journey.

Q: That's truly inspiring! How can people engage with APU and delve deeper into your teachings?
A: While in-person consultations with me are currently limited for safety reasons, APU warmly welcomes individuals who resonate with our mission. If you are connected to someone already affiliated with me, they can serve as your reference to become part of our vibrant community.

Remember: Dr. Wisdom Zerit Teklay is more than just a doctor of natural medicine. He's a visionary, a healer, and a global citizen who firmly believes in the power of each individual to contribute to a better world. Let this Q&A be your starting point on a transformative journey of natural healing, self-discovery, and global impact. Embrace your inner power. Explore the world of Dr. Wisdom Zerit Teklay and APU (Amazoxa Peace University).

CHAPTER 6

DR. WISDOM ZERIT TEKLAY SPEECH

My friends, colleagues, fellow dreamers:
I am Dr. Wisdom Zerit Teklay, not just the president of Amazoxa Peace University, but a bridge-builder, a truth-seeker, and a philosopher. I believe in the power of education, the wisdom of peace, and the fundamental truth that everyone deserves good health, equality, and justice. Labels do not define me. I do not align myself with political parties. I am Amazoxa Peace University, an institution created by the people, for the people. Our vision represents the very essence of Zerit-Tonianism:

1. **Wisdom is the ultimate education.** It's not about degrees or diplomas, but about understanding that fuels compassion, the courage to challenge, and the heart to heal.
2. **True success isn't measured in titles.** It's the quiet strength of being your own champion of peace, the unwavering belief that love conquers conflict.
3. Peace, justice, equality, and good health are not just

ideals. They are the birthright of every soul, the foundation upon which we can build a world where no government, leader, or individual stands above the law.

I understand the complexities of our world, the mixture of hope and despair. Yet, I also know the power of a single voice, a single action, a single word. That is why I carefully choose my words, each one a pebble creating ripples of change in our collective consciousness.

I am not here to sugarcoat reality. I am here to challenge it, to inspire a future where "becoming your own doctor" is more than a metaphor, but a call to action. A future where self-care, mental well-being, and the wisdom within each of us take precedence. This, my friends, is the essence of Zerit-Tonian Nutrition. It is not a passing trend, but a philosophy of nourishment that empowers individuals to listen to their bodies, make conscious choices, and claim their right to a healthy and vibrant life.

Some may call me idealistic, a dreamer lost in the clouds. But I say, let us dream together! Let us imagine a world where peace is not just a fragile dove, but a soaring eagle, its wings outstretched to protect every child, family, and nation. This is my promise to you, my fellow dreamers. I will be your voice, your bridge, your champion. I will fight for a world where Amazoxa Peace University is not merely a name, but a living testament to the power of unity, education, and the unwavering belief that good always triumphs over evil.

Let us embark on this journey together, not as Republicans, Democrats, or Independents, but as a united force for a better tomorrow - Amazoxa. May Zerit-Tonianism be blessed, may Amazoxa Peace University flourish, and may the entire world be filled with blessings.

And now, let's take a moment away from the formalities, a chance to let my heart speak freely without the constraints of podiums and protocols. I am human, fallible, and prone to stumble over a word or thought. But know this: every utterance, every misstep, is fueled by the unwavering belief that words matter, actions matter, and together, we can build a world where peace is not just a dream, but our living reality. So, let us dream, let us laugh, let us stumble and rise again. In this shared journey, in the beautiful messiness of humanity, lies the true magic of Amazoxa, the champion of peace, education, and your well-being.

Thank you.

Dr. Wisdom Zerit Teklay: Championing Peace Through Education and Wisdom

Introduction

My friends, colleagues, fellow dreamers, I stand before you today not just as the president of Amazoxa Peace University, but as a fellow traveler on the path to a brighter future. A future woven from the threads of peace, equality, justice, and good health for all.

A Philosophy for a Better World

My guiding light is a philosophy I call Zerit-Tonianism. It whispers that wisdom, not wealth or power, is the truest measure of success. It reminds me that the champion of peace wears a nobler crown than the champion of war. And it echoes the fundamental truth that no one, not even the president, stands above the law.

Beyond Labels: Embracing Unity

I am not here to claim a political allegiance. I am not Republican, Democrat, or Independent. I am Amazoxa Peace University, a beacon for all who yearn for a world transformed. Our mission statement, etched in our very soul, is a promise: "Peace, Equality, Justice, and Good Health for All."

Words as Seeds of Change

I believe that our words hold immense power, capable of planting seeds of change within ourselves and others. That's why I strive for every syllable to embody the values I hold dear. And why I humbly apologize if, in my unyielding pursuit of truth, I utter a word that causes offense.

Dreams Unbound by Fear

I dream of a world where no word spoken in pursuit of a better tomorrow is used against us. Where self-defense in the courtroom isn't a necessity, but a birthright. I dream, and I hope, that you will join me in making those dreams a reality.

A Call to Action

Let us be the champions of peace, not through empty rhetoric, but through the transformative power of education, self-reliance, and unwavering compassion. Let us be the generation that breaks the chains of division and builds bridges of understanding. Together, let us weave a tapestry of wisdom, where every thread sings the anthem of a world united.

May God bless Zerit-Tonianism, may God bless Amazoxa Peace University, and may God bless the entire world.

End of Formal Speech (Informal Speech Begins)

Now, let's set formality aside and let our hearts speak. I'm no polished orator, just a dreamer with a megaphone. Forgive my stumbles, my unfiltered passion. Just know that every word stems from a place of genuine hope.

(Continue speaking without a script. Share personal anecdotes, aspirations, anything that connects with your audience on a deeper level.)

(End of Informal Speech)

God bless Zerit-Tonianism, God bless Amazoxa Peace University, and may God bless the entire world.

Dr. Wisdom Zerit Teklay: Championing Peace, One Word at a Time

My fellow Americans, I stand before you not as a Republican, Democrat, or Independent. I stand before you as Dr. Wisdom Zerit Teklay, President of Amazoxa Peace University, and a champion for peace.

My philosophy, Zerit-Tonianism, whispers a simple truth: wisdom is the highest form of education, and peace its greatest triumph. It reminds me, with every breath I take, to weave peace, equality, justice, and good health into every word I speak.

I am a bridge, not a barrier. I believe in the power of checks and balances, the grand American ideal where no one, not even the president, stands above the law. This is the very foundation of Amazoxa Peace University, a beacon of learning for the people, by the people, and to the people.

My name, Wisdom, carries the weight of my mission. But sometimes, I dream of a name woven from the threads of our shared aspirations: Peace, Equality, Justice, and Good Health for All. Because these are the words that bind us, across party lines, across borders, across the very fabric of humanity.

My inspiration? It's the audacity of an idea born on American soil: everyone is equal under the law. This is the fertile ground where Amazoxa Project A1 blooms, a project dedicated to nurturing a world where peace paints the canvas of our existence.

I am not here to impress with titles. I am here to impress upon you the power of your own voice. Words are our weapons, but they can also be our shields. Choose them wisely, wield them with compassion, and let them resonate with the Zerit-Tonian truth: Becoming your own doctor is the highest form of self-care.

Let peace be the champion we raise, not war. Let these words be my oath, my promise, my revolution.

(Informal Speech Begins)

Now, let's shed the formalities and speak from the heart. I'm human, and sometimes my tongue trips. Please forgive me if I stumble, if a word escapes unbidden and wounds an ear. My dreams are grand, perhaps even audacious. I dream of directing a film called "The Champion of Peace," a collaboration with giants like Ryan Coogler, Steven Spielberg, and Kathryn Bigelow. I dream of a world where Amazoxa Peace University echoes in every corner, a testament to the collective will for a better tomorrow. But I also dream small. I dream of quiet mornings, of laughter shared with loved ones, of a world where good health isn't a privilege, but a birthright.

May these dreams not be held against me. May they be the fuel that propels me forward, the North Star that guides me through the storms. And when the day dawns and my dreams take flight, remember, it all began with a simple choice: to speak with purpose, to act with kindness, to be the champion of peace, one

CHAPTER 7

ZERIT-TONIANISM: TRANSCENDING THE ISMS FOR A WORLD UNITED IN WISDOM, PEACE, AND EQUALITY

Zerit-Tonianism: A Philosophy for a United and Thriving Planet Earth

Transcending the limitations of existing ideologies, Zerit-Tonianism emerges not as an "-ism" but as a "-ianism." This subtle shift in language signifies a profound departure from the divisive and exclusionary nature of traditional "-isms." Zerit-

Tonianism isn't about clinging to rigid systems or worshiping dogmatic leaders; it's about embracing the boundless potential of humanity united. Imagine a world where:

Wisdom reigns supreme: Education fosters critical thinking, empathy, and a thirst for knowledge. Success isn't measured by material wealth, but by the depth of one's understanding and the positive impact they create.
Peace prevails: Not as the fragile absence of conflict, but as a vibrant tapestry woven from justice, equality, and respect for all beings. Warmongering is no longer glorified; the true champions are those who build bridges and heal wounds.
A healthy planet nourishes healthy people: Zerit-Tonian Nutrition, a cornerstone of the philosophy, emphasizes holistic well-being, environmental consciousness, and responsible consumption. We become stewards of the Earth, not plunderers.

Dr. Wisdom Zerit Teklay, the visionary architect of Zerit-Tonianism, eloquently declares: "Zerit-Tonianism isn't confined by the labels of 'Amazoxan,' 'Planet-Earthian,' or any other earthly identifier. It's a universal language, a beacon of hope for a species yearning for unity and progress." Instead of division, Zerit-Tonianism embraces:

Unionism: Recognizing the interconnectedness of all beings and nations, we stand together, not against each other.
Diversitynianism: A kaleidoscope of cultures, ethnicities, and perspectives enriches the human experience. We celebrate our differences, learning and growing from each other.
Minimalistinianism: Contentment replaces consumerism. We value experiences over possessions, finding joy in the simple beauty of life.
Unclassiflednianism of information: Knowledge empowers. Transparency and open access to information are the bedrock

of informed decision-making and collective progress.

Zerit-Tonianism isn't a utopian dream; it's a call to action. It's about actively building a world where:

Leadership inspires, not dominates.
Quality trumps quantity in all aspects of life.
Teams collaborate, not compete, for the greater good.
Inclusion, not exclusion, becomes the norm.
Reconciliation heals the wounds of the past, fostering a brighter future.

This isn't just a philosophy; it's a movement. Join Dr. Wisdom Zerit Teklay at Amazoxa Peace University, embrace Zerit-Tonianism, and let's co-create a world where peace, justice, and well-being are not distant aspirations, but our lived reality. Remember, the highest level of success is wisdom. Let's choose to be the champions of peace, together.

Zerit-Tonianism: A Philosophy Transcending Division

Not a doctrine, but a compass. Zerit-Tonianism isn't a rigid set of rules, but a dynamic philosophy guiding us towards a brighter future. It's not about subscribing to an "ism," but embracing a set of guiding principles that transcend labels and unite us. Beyond the limitations. Zerit-Tonianism rejects the limitations of existing ideologies. It's not Capitalism, Socialism, or any other ism that confines us to pre-defined boxes. It's about forging a new path, one that prioritizes:

Wisdom over war. Zerit-Tonianism champions peacemakers, not warmongers. True success lies in understanding, not domination.
A united Planet Earth. We are not separate nations, but one global community. Our borders are not lines on a map, but the

embrace of our shared humanity.

Equality and justice for all. No one is above the law, not even the president. Every voice deserves to be heard, every right deserves to be protected.

A symphony of cultures. Diversity is not a hurdle, but a source of strength. We celebrate the richness of our differences, weaving them into a tapestry of vibrant unity.

Good health, a universal blessing. Well-being is not a privilege, but a fundamental right. Zerit-Tonianism champions healthy communities, nourished by knowledge and mindful living.

A philosophy in action. Dr. Wisdom Zerit Teklay, the philosopher behind Zerit-Tonianism, isn't just a dreamer; he's a builder. Amazoxa Peace University embodies his vision, where education empowers and leadership inspires. Embrace the "nianisms" within. Zerit-Tonianism isn't a singular entity, but a constellation of guiding principles. Each "nianism" â€" from Minimalism to Unclassification â€" represents a facet of a greater whole. They are not restrictions, but pathways to a more fulfilling existence. Join the movement. Zerit-Tonianism isn't a spectator sport. It's a call to action. Be a champion for peace, a voice for equality, a builder of bridges. Let's rewrite the narrative, not with labels and divisions, but with shared values and collective action. Zerit-Tonianism: not an "ism," but a compass. A philosophy for a world ready to evolve, ready to unite, ready to thrive.

Zerit-Tonianism: A Philosophy Beyond Isms

Not an ism, but an ism-ism. Zerit-Tonianism isn't confined by the limitations of existing ideologies. It's a philosophy that transcends the labels, the divisions, the us-versus-them narratives that have plagued humanity for far too long. Imagine a world where:

Wisdom reigns supreme. Education isn't just about memorizing facts; it's about cultivating discernment, compassion, and the ability to see the bigger picture.
Peace isn't a fragile dream, but a living reality. Conflicts are resolved not through force, but through understanding, empathy, and a shared commitment to justice.
Equality isn't a right, but a birthright. Every person, regardless of their background, beliefs, or origin, deserves to be valued and empowered.
Good health isn't a privilege, but a fundamental human right. Access to clean water, nutritious food, and preventive care is a cornerstone, not a luxury.

Zerit-Tonianism is the philosophy for:

The Amazoxan: A global citizen, united by shared values and a commitment to building a better future for all.
The Planet-Earther: Someone who understands that we are all interconnected, and that caring for our home is not an option, but an imperative.
The Unionist: A bridge-builder, fostering cooperation and collaboration across cultures, communities, and even galaxies.
The Peacefulist: A warrior of dialogue, wielding words and empathy instead of weapons.
The Equalitynian: A champion of fairness, ensuring that opportunity and dignity are not just ideals, but lived experiences.

It's not about blind acceptance, but about conscious engagement. Zerit-Tonianism encourages healthy debate, critical thinking, and the courage to challenge the status quo. It's about questioning, evolving, and refining the path towards a more just and harmonious world. It's not about blind optimism, but about pragmatic idealism. Zerit-Tonianism acknowledges the challenges, the complexities, the darkness that still lingers. But it also believes in the power of collective action, in the boundless potential within each of us to create a brighter tomorrow. Zerit-Tonianism is not a destination, but a journey. It's a constant striving, a learning process, a commitment to keep moving forward, hand in hand, towards the horizon where wisdom, peace, and equality illuminate the path for all. Join us. Let's rewrite the ism-ism. Let's be Zerit-Tonians

CHAPTER 8

WRITE SOMETHING WORTH READING: A MANIFESTO FOR AUTHORS IN A NOISY WORLD

Compelling, Influential, Powerful: Dr. Wisdom Zerit Teklayâ€™s Message
Open with a bang, quoting the iconic Benjamin Franklin: "In a world saturated with words, Dr. Wisdom Zerit Teklay challenges us: 'Write something worth reading, or do something worth writing about.' This isn't just a call to action; it's a gauntlet thrown down to every aspiring author, every seeker of truth."
Intrigue with the mystery of stolen ideas: "Dr. Wisdom Zerit Teklay, a pioneer in both philosophy and nutrition, warns

of 'idea thieves' lurking in the publishing shadows. He urges authors to encrypt their manuscripts, to be the sole guardians of their genius. This isn't paranoia; it's a strategic manifesto for protecting your intellectual property in a ruthless marketplace."

Highlight Zerit-Tonianism's core principles: "Peace, justice, equality, good health for all. No one is above the law. These aren't mere platitudes; they're the bedrock of Dr. Wisdom Zerit Teklayâ€™s philosophy, the driving force behind his relentless pursuit of a better world."

Emphasize the joy of unfiltered expression: "Experience the freedom of crafting your book without government censorship or societal pressures. Dr. Wisdom Zerit Teklay doesn't just advocate for this freedom; he embodies it. He finds his happiness not in bestseller lists, but in the unadulterated creation of his vision."

Offer practical tools for aspiring authors: "Turn off the noise. Silence the TV, social media, and even your own internal chatter. Allow your original thoughts to flourish in the fertile silence. Focus on completing what you've started, harness your emotions, and let truth be your guiding light. These aren't restrictions; they are the keys to unlocking your authentic voice."

End with a powerful image: "Every word you write, Dr. Wisdom Zerit Teklay reminds us, is a seed. Plant them with care, for they have the power to nourish a world yearning for peace, equality, and good health. Will you join him in cultivating this garden of change? Driven Writing: A Manifesto for Authors in a Noisy World."

Open with a spark: Instead of starting with a lengthy quote, capture the reader's attention with a captivating question or a bold statement that encapsulates the essence of the book. For example: Dr. Wisdom Zerit Teklay's groundbreaking message.

Follow with a powerful hook: Introduce Dr. Wisdom Zerit Teklayâ€™s quote about "writing something worth reading." Briefly mention Benjamin Franklin and then transition to the book's purpose: Dr. Wisdom Zerit Teklay's mission.

Condense the warnings: Merge the two quotes about protecting your ideas and editing. Emphasize the importance of self-reliance and critical thinking in the publishing process. Dr. Wisdom Zerit Teklay's advice.

Highlight the Zerit-Tonian philosophy: Rather than using bullet points, weave the core principles into a narrative that aligns with the book's theme. Dr. Wisdom Zerit Teklay's guiding principles.

Celebrate the joy of independent creation: Capture the liberating feeling of writing without external pressures. This book is for those who dare to embrace their uniqueness. Dr. Wisdom Zerit Teklay's celebration of creativity.

Offer practical advice: Transform the "turn-off-everything" quote into actionable steps. Frame these as tools for cultivating focus and avoiding distractions. Dr. Wisdom Zerit Teklay's practical guidance.

End with a call to action: Allow the reader to glimpse the transformative power of their own voice. Dr. Wisdom Zerit Teklay's rallying cry.

Proofread:
- Ensure smooth transitions between sections.
- Consider replacing overly technical terms with simpler alternatives.
- Check for typos and grammatical inconsistencies.

By incorporating these suggestions, you can transform your content into a compelling manifesto that inspires readers to embrace their own "Driven Writing."

CHAPTER 9

WISDOM AND PEACE: THE QUOTES OF DR. WISDOM ZERIT TEKLAY

Can Wisdom Conquer War? Dr. Wisdom Zerit Teklay's Radical Proposal

About Dr. Wisdom Zerit Teklay: Dr. Wisdom Zerit Teklay is a visionary philosopher, educator, and global citizen committed to promoting peace, justice, and equality. As the esteemed president of Amazoxa Peace University, he leads a groundbreaking institution that fosters global peace through education and dialogue. Guided by his profound Zerit-Tonianism philosophy, Dr. Wisdom Zerit Teklay advocates for wisdom as the pinnacle of education and champions the values of peace, justice, and personal responsibility for the betterment of our world.

Zerit-Tonianism: Wisdom for a Better World

Zerit-Tonianism is not just a philosophy; it is a transformative blueprint for a brighter future. It firmly believes in the power of wisdom to guide our actions and shape our world. In an era overshadowed by wars and inequalities, Zerit-Tonianism stands as a beacon of hope, reminding us that peace, justice, and personal well-being should be our collective goals. It exhorts us to rise above the destructive forces of war and injustice and embrace a future guided by wisdom, equality, and global well-being.

Quotes on Peace and Global Solutions:

- "Wisdom is the highest level of education. Success is measured by wisdom. Being a champion of peace is wiser than being a champion of war."
- "World War is the greatest problem plaguing our world today. Solving a major world war is not solely the duty of governments but the responsibility of every individual. Let us prevent any major world war by adopting peaceful approaches and diplomatic solutions rather than resorting to arms, nuclear bombs, and cyber-attacks."
- "A global constitution unites us all."
- "Sanctioning a country represents the highest

and truest form of global dictatorship our world has ever witnessed. The greatest tragedy of sanctioning a country lies in the innocent people who suffer due to their nation's sanctions, not the government of the sanctioning country itself."

Quotes on Individual Empowerment and Self-Care:
- "Becoming your own doctor is the ultimate level of self-help therapy."
- "The highest form of self-care is becoming the primary care doctor of your own mind, body, and emotions."

Quotes on Human Potential and the Future:
- "No matter how advanced artificial intelligence becomes, it will always depend on human intelligence to function. Artificial intelligence without human intelligence is like a car without an engine."
- "When Barack Obama became the first African American President of the United States, it ignited my ambition and hope to witness a naturalized American citizen becoming President, regardless of their birthplace."

Dr. Wisdom Zerit Teklay's message resonates with hope, responsibility, and an unwavering belief in the power of collective action. His quotes inspire us to embrace wisdom, challenge injustice, and work together to build a more peaceful and equitable world.

About Dr. Wisdom Zerit Teklay:

As the esteemed president of Amazoxa Peace University, Dr. Wisdom Zerit Teklay stands at the forefront of promoting peace, justice, and human potential. His multifaceted roles as the philosopher of Zerit-Tonianism and Zerit-Tonian Nutrition reflect his commitment to empowering individuals and fostering global unity.

- **President of Amazoxa Peace University:** A unique institution dedicated to fostering global peace through education and dialogue.

- **Philosopher of Zerit-Tonianism:** Founder of a philosophy emphasizing wisdom, self-reliance, and global unity.
- **Philosopher of Zerit-Tonian Nutrition:** A passionate advocate for healthy eating for a healthier world.

Dr. Wisdom Zerit's quotes offer insightful perspectives on various global issues, urging us to reflect and take action.

On Wisdom and Success:

Dr. Wisdom Zerit Teklay reminds us that true success lies not only in external achievements but also in inner growth and self-awareness. He emphasizes the importance of taking responsibility for our well-being and seeking knowledge to navigate life's challenges.

On Peace and Global Responsibility:

Dr. Wisdom Zerit Teklay passionately advocates for global peace, urging individuals and governments alike to share the responsibility. He envisions a world where everyone is treated equally, governed by justice, and free from conflict.

On Challenging the Status Quo:

Dr. Wisdom Zerit Teklay boldly criticizes practices such as sanctions and invasions, highlighting their detrimental impact on innocent civilians. He calls for alternative solutions based on mutual respect and understanding.

On Human Potential and Technology:

Dr. Wisdom Zerit Teklay firmly believes in the boundless potential of human intelligence. He sees technology as a tool, not a replacement, and encourages us to nurture our unique cognitive abilities for the betterment of humanity.

A Call to Action:

Dr. Wisdom Zerit's quotes are not mere pronouncements; they are passionate calls to action. He invites us to embrace wisdom, advocate for peace, challenge injustice, and cultivate our human potential. His Zerit-Tonianism philosophy offers a roadmap towards a more just, peaceful, and equitable world. Let us heed his words and work together to create the world that Dr. Wisdom Zerit Teklay envisions: a world where wisdom reigns, peace prevails, and humanity thrives.

About Dr. Zerit Teklay Sebhatleab:

Dr. Wisdom Zerit Teklay is a multi-faceted individual with a passion for peace and a dedication to human progress. As the President of Amazoxa Peace University, the philosopher behind Zerit-Tonianism, and a champion of Zerit-Tonian Nutrition, he tirelessly works towards a world free from conflict and suffering.

Quotes:

- **Wisdom as the Pinnacle of Education: undefined**
- **Unlocking Success through Problem-Solving: undefined**
- **Preventing World Wars: A Shared Responsibility: undefined**
- **Unity Beyond Differences: undefined**
- **The Pitfalls of Power: undefined**

"Sanctioning a country or invading an autonomous country are part of the problem, not part of the solution of keeping peace."

CHAPTER 10

RECLAIMING DEMOCRACY: A ZERIT-TONIAN MANIFESTO FOR A JUST WORLD

Seeds of Freedom: Planting True Democracy in a Barren World Reclaiming Democracy: A Call to Action from the Zerit-Tonian Perspective Have you ever felt your voice silenced, your vote ignored? Do you yearn for a world where peace, justice, and equality transcend meaningless rhetoric? This is the world envisioned by Dr. Wisdom Zerit Teklay, the eminent philosopher of Zerit-Tonianism and President of Amazoxa Peace University. He calls it true democracy, a powerful antidote to the facade of freedom that pervades our global society. According to Dr. Wisdom Teklay, true democracy is not about the accumulation

of power, but rather about its responsible exercise. It is not about suppressing dissent, but rather amplifying diverse voices. It is not about exploiting the vulnerable, but rather empowering them. This vision lays the foundation for a society where peace becomes the ultimate triumph, justice reigns supreme, and equality becomes an inherent right rather than a privilege. Regrettably, Dr. Teklay reveals that this utopia currently exists nowhere on Earth. We witness powerful nations manipulating the destiny of weaker ones under the guise of humanitarian intervention. Leaders amass wealth while their people suffer in poverty, their voices drowned out by the relentless clamor of military might. Constitutions are treated as malleable suggestions, with principles sacrificed at the altar of self-interest. This is a far cry from the legacy we were promised; it is not the future we deserve. Dr. Wisdom Zerit Teklay offers a lifeline, a philosophy interwoven with the tenets of Zerit-Tonianism: - Wisdom is the highest form of education. Let us seek understanding, not blind obedience. - Peace supersedes war. Let dialogue be our weapon to disarm conflict, not bombs. - Justice must be blind, not selective. No one, not even the most powerful, should stand above the law. - Equality is the bedrock of society, not an exception. Every voice, every vote, holds significance. These principles are not mere ideals; they are actionable principles. Dr. Teklay presents a profound contrast to the artificial democracy we have come to accept: - True democracy emphasizes cooperation, not invasion. - True democracy amplifies the voices of its citizens, not silences them. - True democracy empowers the marginalized, rather than exploiting their vulnerability. Dr. Teklay reminds us that the power to effect change lies within each of us. We, the people, are the authors of our own destiny. The evidence is clear: - The rising stars of true democracy, such as Martin Luther King Jr. and Malcolm X, faced suppression for daring to challenge the status quo. - Billions are spent on expanding military bases in foreign lands, while core components of society, like healthcare and education, crumble at home. - Governments subject their own citizens to surveillance, treating them as suspects rather than constituents. This is not the future we are willing to accept. This is not the legacy we will leave for our children. Dr. Wisdom Zerit Teklay's call to action echoes in the hearts of those yearning for change: - Rise with informed voices, not weapons. Let peaceful protest be our rallying cry. - Demand transparency, accountability, and a return to first principles. Let the constitution be our shield. - Plant the seeds of change, one vote, one conversation, one act of courage at a time. Let our actions become our manifesto. This is our moment, our opportunity to shape our legacy. Let us rewrite the narrative, not with bloodshed, but with the power of pen and ink. It is time to reclaim democracy, not from tyrants, but from our own complacency. Together, let us build a world that honors the very essence of true democracy. Join the movement. Plant the seeds. Let freedom bloom. Reclaiming Democracy: A Zerit-Tonian Manifesto for a Just World We're tired of whispers swallowed by drones. We're weary of "artificial democracy" parading as true freedom. We yearn for a world where peace, justice, and equality are not mere whispers but the resounding cries of our generation. Dr. Wisdom Zerit Teklay, the philosopher of Zerit-Tonianism and President of Amazoxa Peace University, paints a vivid vision - a vision of true democracy that stands in stark contrast to the empty promises and hollow echoes that we have come to accept. According to Dr. Wisdom Zerit Teklay, true democracy is not about exerting control or suppressing dissent. It is about wielding power with respect and amplifying the voices of the marginalized. It is about empowering the vulnerable, rather than exploiting their weaknesses. This is the bedrock of a society where peace is not an elusive dream, but the ultimate triumph. It is a society where justice reigns supreme, and equality is not a privilege, but a birthright. However, this utopia remains elusive. Dr. Wisdom Zerit Teklay reveals that true democracy is nowhere to be found on Earth. We witness powerful nations dictating the fate of weaker ones, disguising their actions as humanitarian interventions. We see leaders accumulating great wealth while their people suffer in poverty, their cries drowned out by the menacing roar of military machinery. We observe constitutions treated as mere suggestions, with principles trampled upon in the pursuit of self-interest. This is not the legacy we were promised. This is not the future we accept. This is not the world we will leave for our children. In the face of these challenges, Dr. Teklay offers a lifeline â€" a philosophy rooted in Zerit-Tonianism: - Wisdom is the highest form of education. Let us seek understanding, rather than blind obedience. - Peace should triumph over war. Let dialogue disarm conflicts, not bombs. - Justice must be blind, impartial and universal. No one, regardless of their power, should stand above the law. - Equality is not a privilege for the few, but the cornerstone of a just society. Every voice, every vote, matters. These principles are not lofty ideals to be admired from a distance; they are actionable principles that guide our actions. Dr. Teklay's vision of true democracy offers a stark contrast to the artificial democracy that surrounds us: - True democracy does not invade foreign lands, but extends a hand of friendship. - True democracy does not silence its citizens, but amplifies their cries for justice. - True democracy does not exploit the weak, but empowers the marginalized. Dr. Teklay reminds us that the seeds of change lie within each of us. It is the people who hold the power. We are the authors of our own destiny. The evidence is clear: - The rising stars of true democracy, like Martin Luther King Jr. and Malcolm X, were silenced for daring to challenge the status quo. - Billions are spent on expanding military bases in foreign lands, while the foundations of society, such as healthcare and education, crumble at home. - Governments betray their own citizens, treating them as suspects rather than constituents. This is not the future we accept. This is not the world we will leave for our children. Dr. Wisdom Zerit Teklay's call to action resonates with those yearning for change: - Rise with informed voices, not weapons. Let peaceful protest be our battle cry. - Demand transparency, accountability, and a return to first principles. Let the constitution be our shield. - Plant the seeds of change, through each vote, each conversation, each act of courage. Let our actions speak louder than words. This is our moment, our opportunity to shape our legacy. Let us rewrite the narrative, not with the bloodshed of conflict, but with the ink of our collective will. Let us reclaim democracy, not from tyrants, but from our own complacency. Together, let us build a world that lives up to the ideals of true democracy. Join the movement. Plant the seeds. Let freedom bloom. This is not just a manifesto; it is a call to arms. A call to whisper truth louder than the drones that silence us. A call to plant seeds of justice in the cracks of a broken system. A call to rise with informed voices and demand the world we deserve. Let freedom bloom.

CHAPTER 11

THE UNIVERSITY OF EXPERIENCE: WHERE REAL LEARNING BEGINS

Experience: Unleash Your Full Potential

Experience is not just a word, it is the foundation of true education. It is a transformative journey that shapes us, imparting invaluable lessons along the way. In a world that is constantly evolving, there is nothing quite like the wisdom gained through firsthand experience. Life itself is a vast university, with its campuses spread across every corner of the globe. Here, you have the unique opportunity to embark on a self-paced, self-taught education that is open to all. And the best part? Experience itself is the most exceptional professor you will ever encounter. This university is renowned for its prestige, its rigorous demands, and its unparalleled rewards. By earning your degree in experience, you will become the most educated person you know, setting yourself apart from the rest.

While formal education certainly has its place, it cannot replicate the real-life lessons that experience offers. The ability to read and write is the only true prerequisite for success, in my opinion. Throughout history, countless examples exist of world-changing inventions and innovations brought to life by individuals who defied traditional education systems – myself included. When you choose the path less traveled, you unlock the freedom to explore your full potential. The University of Experience empowers you to tap into your authentic self, igniting the magic that lies within. It's not just about acquiring facts and figures; it's about forging your own unique path through the trials and triumphs of life.

While schools may teach you to read and write, they cannot provide you with the wisdom and experience that come from living life to the fullest. They may offer theories, dates, and formulas – all valuable in their own right – but they pale in comparison to the raw, unfiltered lessons learned in the real world. Life's ups and downs serve as the ultimate crash course, offering the most authentic and impactful education you can receive. So why settle for knowledge without experience, when you can embrace the true power of both?

Let the whispers of history remind you of the brilliant minds who defied the confines of textbooks and pursued their dreams. They may have dropped out of conventional education, but they never stopped learning. They graduated with flying colors from the University of Experience, forever changing the world with their innovative ideas. So, why follow the conventional path? Embrace the transformative power of experience. Let life be your teacher, guiding you towards a future filled with limitless possibilities. The University of Experience is the only degree worth having – are you ready to embark on the journey of a lifetime? Welcome to the University of Life: Where Experience is the True Educator.

CHAPTER 12

A CLARION CALL FOR PEACE: HUMBLE LEADERSHIP IN A DIVIDED WORLD

A Humble Call for Global Transformation: Let Peace Prevail
Esteemed Leaders of the World's Superpower Nations,
As I, Dr. Wisdom Zerit Teklay, the dedicated CEO of Amazoxa Peace University, pen this letter, I do so with a fervent plea for universal peace, justice, and prosperity. I invite you to **step away from the self-assumed role of global law enforcement.**Such a position threatens to incite an unprecedented backlash.
Honorable Commanders, may I propose a thought? Imagine **granting foreign nations their sovereignty by retracting your military bases from their landscapes.** This gesture of respect and trust would forge a path of gratitude in the hearts of these nations.
Rather than being symbols of conflict, invasion, sanctions, and the consequences they bear, **take up the noble cause of**

peace. Impart lessons of humility, not superiority, to your future generations. As a humble servant of education, I, Dr. Wisdom Zerit Teklay, proudly champion this cause.

At Amazoxa Peace Global University, we've designed an innovative curriculum, "Be Humble," to breathe life into this precious virtue.

Dr. Wisdom Zerit Teklay,

President of Amazoxa Peace University, Advocate of Zerit-Tonianism and Zerit-Tonian Nutrition

The Philosophy of Zerit-Tonianism posits:
- Wisdom stands as the ultimate milestone of education and success.
- Embracing peace triumphs over fostering war.
- Peace, justice, equality, and good health are rights for all.
- No administration or official is exempt from the law; compliance is mandatory for all, including presidents.

May the blessings of God fill Zerit-Tonianism/Zerit-Tonian Nutrition and Amazoxa Peace University. Driven by the guiding principles of Amazoxa, the world will bloom in unparalleled prosperity.

With utmost respect,

Dr. Wisdom Zerit Teklay, CEO and President of Amazoxa Peace University

Representing the Board Members of the United Countries of the World Government Amazoxa Committee

Date: April 10, 2022

A Call to Global Leadership: The Power of Humble Stewardship

This letter, penned by Dr. Wisdom Zerit Teklay, CEO of Amazoxa Peace University, serves as an urgent appeal to the leaders of the world's superpowers. She calls for a transition from the role of assumed global police to advocates for peace. Dr. Teklay champions this transformation, encouraging leaders to take up the mantle of humility and collaboration, a value deeply woven into our "Be Humble" curriculum.

The letter underscores the potential dangers of "super

powerism," urging leaders to consider a shift towards self-governance and mutual respect. Dr. Teklay visualizes a world where nations are free to shape their own destinies, unhampered by foreign military presence.

Dr. Teklay's call to action extends beyond non-intervention; it is an active plea for peacebuilding. She urges superpowers to advocate for justice, equality, and health for all, ensuring legal accountability across the board. By adhering to these principles, she believes that the world can flourish under Amazoxa Peace University's guidance, ushering in an era of unprecedented global prosperity.

This plea is more than just a letter; it's a call-to-action, challenging existing norms and proposing a future built on humility, cooperation, and shared humanity.

Final Thoughts: A Global Call for Humility and Peaceful Coexistence

Esteemed Commanders of the World's Superpowers,

Your power is undeniable, yet true might is characterized by humility and compassion. Choose to illuminate the path of peace, instead of fostering conflict. Teach our youth not the language of superiority, but the dialogue of understanding and cooperation.

Visualize a future where our military bases blossom into learning institutions, where sanctions pave the way for bridges of unity, where trust douses the sparks of fear. This is the future envisioned by Amazoxa Peace University—a world revolving around collaboration rather than competition, where wisdom is held in the highest regard.

Join us in this transformative journey, and let Amazoxa spearhead a global shift, making "Zerit-Tonianism" not just a philosophy, but a lifestyle. Together, let's shape a world where peace, justice, and equality are our shared reality, not just a distant dream.

This is more than a plea; it is a call to action. Rise above individual gains and embrace our shared humanity. The era of "super powerism" is waning. Now is the time for global peace.

Yours sincerely,
Dr. Zerit Teklay Sebhatleab
CEO and President, Amazoxa Peace University

A Plea for Peaceful Transformation: Upholding the Reign of Peace

As the dawn of a new age beckons, we, the advocates of the Future Global Constitution, beseech the world's leaders to seize this transformative opportunity. Abandon the restricting shackles of "super powerism" and adopt the role of champions for universal peace, justice, and prosperity.

Remember, true strength lies not in the might of armies, but in the wisdom of choosing peace over conflict, humility over arrogance. By vacating your military bases and empowering nations to govern themselves, you plant the seeds of a future that values every voice, every culture, and every life.

Let Amazoxa Peace University guide you on this journey. Through the transformative power of education, we can nurture a generation enriched by the principles of Zerit-Tonianism: where wisdom reigns supreme, equality blossoms, and law upholds all.

Join us, dear leaders, in fostering a world where children learn the power of humility rather than the perils of war. Together, let's usher in an era where Amazoxa's vision becomes our collective reality – a world thriving under the banner of peace, where every nation, every individual can reach their ultimate potential.

This plea is not just a request; it is a heartfelt invocation for a future where humanity transcends divisions and writes a new chapter of unity, harmony, and boundless progress.

The decision lies with you, leaders of the world. Will you walk the path of humility and peace or cling to the fading remnants of an outdated power structure? The world awaits your response.

CHAPTER 13

THE NEVER-SICK: THE BODY ELECTRIC: UNPLUG FROM PILLS, POWER UP WITH PLANTS

The Plant-Fueled Revolution: Ditch the Drugs, Ignite Your Immunity

Why do we get sick? It's a question that has puzzled humanity for centuries. We've searched for answers in pills, surgeries, and complex theories. But what if the solution is simpler than we think?

Welcome to the world of Dr. Wisdom Zerit Teklay, a man who has never experienced illness in his entire life. His secret? A plant-based lifestyle, mindful living, and a deep understanding of his body's needs.

Let me introduce you to the pillars of Dr. Wisdom's never-sick life:

- **Plant Power:** Dr. Wisdom believes in the healing power of plants. He avoids processed foods, junk food, and GMO animal products, choosing instead to nourish himself with a vibrant array of organic fruits, vegetables, and whole grains.
- **Hydration Hero:** Water is his elixir of life. He stays away from alcohol and sugary drinks, favoring the pure, natural taste of water and homemade milk.
- **Sleep Savvy:** Dr. Wisdom understands the importance of rest and rejuvenation. He aims for 6-8 hours of sleep, avoiding oversleeping and never relying on sleeping pills.
- **Stress Slayer:** Dr. Wisdom recognizes the detrimental impact of stress on the immune system. He actively cultivates peace within himself, avoiding negativity and embracing a life of purpose and passion.
- **Mindful Master:** He is the primary care physician of his own life. Dr. Wisdom listens to his body, experiments with natural remedies like his homemade immune-boosting concoction, and trusts his intuition.
- **News Ninja:** He carefully curates his media diet, avoiding negativity and violence, opting instead for inspiring news and the calming beauty of nature documentaries.

But Dr. Wisdom's philosophy extends beyond the physical. He champions social connection and believes that isolation weakens the spirit and the immune system. He is a strong advocate for peace, justice, and equality, recognizing the interconnectedness of well-being and a just world.

Dr. Wisdom's story is not just a testament to the power of plant-based eating. It's a call to action. He urges us to take control of our health, to become our own primary care physicians, to listen to our bodies, and to experiment with natural remedies. He reminds us that prevention is better than cure, and that small changes in our daily habits can lead to a lifetime of health.

So remember:

- Eating plant-based organic food is the mother of good health and longevity.
- Eating plant-based organic food is the best medicine of all time.
- You have the power to heal yourself.

Join Dr. Wisdom Zerit on the path to never-ending health. Embrace the power of plants, the wisdom of your own body, and the incredible potential of a life lived mindfully. May peace, justice, equality, and good health be with you all.

- Dr. Wisdom Zerit Teklay

President, Amazoxa Peace University

Philosopher of Zerit-Tonianism Philosophy and Zerit-Tonian Nutrition

CHAPTER 14

A SEED OF REVOLUTION: LET EDUCATION BLOOM IN THE HEARTS OF THE OPPRESSED

FROM WHISPERS IN ERITREA TO A GLOBAL ROAR: THE

UNSTOPPABLE RISE OF AMAZOXA PEACE UNIVERSITY

Dr. Wisdom Zerit Teklay, CEO and President of Amazoxa Peace University, the Home of True Education, has come to a profound realization: everything in life is a risk. But the greatest risk of all is not taking a risk at all and succumbing to complacency.

Dr. Wisdom Zerit Teklay is taking a monumental risk by establishing Amazoxa Peace University in the face of established and prestigious institutions. These institutions, threatened by Amazoxa's revolutionary approach, may resort to extreme measures to eliminate it. They may even try to silence this beacon of true education by bribing government officials.

However, Dr. Wisdom Zerit Teklay remains undeterred. By sharing the university's ideas and intellectual property with billions of people worldwide, he has planted a seed that cannot be uprooted. Even if he were to fall, his legacy would live on through those who carry the torch of Amazoxa Peace University.

This book serves as Dr. Wisdom Zerit Teklay's will, transferring all his assets, intellectual property, and even cryptocurrency holdings to the ownership of the world's poor. In the event of his untimely demise, whether natural or at the hands of envious rivals, his wealth will become a powerful tool for their advancement.

No government, corporation, or individual will be able to claim this inheritance. The sole beneficiaries are the poor of all nations, forever empowered by Dr. Wisdom Zerit Teklay's

unwavering belief in education, peace, and justice.
This is Dr. Wisdom Zerit Teklay's gamble, his challenge to the status quo, and his ultimate act of faith in humanity.
Signatory:
Dr. Wisdom Zerit Teklay
President, Amazoxa Peace University
Philosopher of Zerit-Tonianism and Zerit-Tonian Nutrition
Witnesses:
Worldwide Amazoxa Peace University Board Members Committee
Risk
Dr. Wisdom Zerit Teklay, CEO and President of Amazoxa Peace University, the Home of True Education, has a radical perspective on risk. He doesn't believe in questioning whether everything is a risk or not. Instead, he posits that everything in life is a risk.
This audacious statement sets the stage for a passionate exploration of the greatest risk of all: not taking a risk and succumbing to complacency. Dr. Wisdom Zerit Teklay exemplifies this daring approach with the introduction and establishment of Amazoxa Peace University, a revolutionary concept poised to disrupt the traditional education landscape.
He acknowledges the formidable adversaries he faces: prestigious universities who might resort to any means to eliminate his "threat." He even anticipates potential bribery and political maneuvering to silence his ideas. Yet, Dr. Wisdom Zerit remains undaunted.
His unwavering confidence stems from a strategic move. He has already sown the seeds of his vision, sending the blueprints of Amazoxa Peace University, its intellectual properties, and his Zerit-Tonian philosophies to billions across the globe. This act ensures that his legacy will endure, even if he faces unforeseen challenges.
Dr. Wisdom Zerit Teklay's philosophy, Zerit-Tonianism, emphasizes the pursuit of wisdom, peace, justice, and equality. He advocates for a world where no one, including leaders,

is above the law. This unwavering belief in universal rights fuels his fight against the established power structures in education.

The most impactful section is Dr. Wisdom Zerit's declaration of his will. He vows to transfer all his assets, intellectual property, and even cryptocurrency holdings to the ownership of the world's poor. This act of selfless generosity stands as a testament to his unwavering commitment to serving the underprivileged.

He addresses the world, particularly the United States, his adopted home. He warns that if he faces an untimely demise, be it natural or orchestrated by envious rivals, his legacy will live on. His books, wealth, and the very idea of Amazoxa Peace University will become the inheritance of the impoverished, a beacon of hope amidst a system he deems inadequate.

Dr. Wisdom Zerit Teklay's message is a potent blend of defiance, idealism, and selflessness. He dares to challenge the status quo, not with aggression, but with the power of transformative education and unwavering faith in humanity's potential. His is a story of audacious risk, unwavering conviction, and a legacy destined to empower the most vulnerable.

Risk

"I, Dr. Wisdom Zerit Teklay, CEO and President of Amazoxa Peace University, the Home of True Education, have learned that the question is not whether everything is a risk or not. It is, instead, what in this life is not a risk? Everything in this thing we call 'life' is a risk. The greatest risk of all time, in the history of risks, is not taking a risk and being complacent.

The greatest risk I am taking right now, in the history of my life journey, is the introduction and establishment of Amazoxa Peace University, the Home of True Education, in the real world of formal education. Why is this a risk?

It is a big risk because prestigious universities that exist today may do whatever it takes to eliminate me and my idea of Amazoxa Peace University. They may even go above and beyond to bribe lobbyists in government offices to eliminate my university's existence from the face of the earth.

Yet, they will fail. I have already planted a seed of an idea, the idea of Amazoxa Peace University, the Home of True Education, in the hearts and minds of billions of people of all nations in the world. I have done this by sending them the PDF file of this book and Amazoxa Peace University ideas and intellectual properties. They will become the beneficiaries of my idea, Amazoxa Peace University, the Home of True Education.

Anyone to whom I have sent the Amazoxa Peace University intellectual properties will continue the legacy of my idea.

Dr. Wisdom Zerit Teklay

President of Amazoxa Peace University; Philosopher of Zerit-Tonianism Philosophy; Philosopher of Zerit-Tonian Nutrition

Dr. Wisdom Zerit Teklay's Zerit-Tonianism Philosophy states that:

"Wisdom is the highest level of Education. The highest level of success is Wisdom. To be the champion of peace is wiser than to be the champion of war. Peace, Justice, Equality, and Good Health for all. No government or government official is above the law; no person is above the law. Everyone, including the president, must obey the law. God Bless Zerit-Tonianism/Zerit-Tonian Nutrition, God Bless Amazoxa Peace Education to prevail in the real world of formal educations. The headquarters of Amazoxa Peace University, the Home of True Education, will forever be in Asmara, Eritrea.

I, Dr. Wisdom Zerit Teklay, CEO and President of Amazoxa Peace University, the Home of True Education, do solemnly swear in front of the Amazoxa Peace University Global Court of Law that I, Dr. Wisdom Zerit Teklay, by my free will and good intention for the greater good of all poor people in the world, am giving my testimony and transfer of my Will of all the assets, intellectual properties, cryptocurrencies, stocks I own, and will have under my name and under the name of my Global Enterprise, Amazoxa Peace University, the Home of True Education, to be under the ownership of all the poor people of all poor countries in the world.

I am publishing my Will in my book for all the World Governments, Corporations, and all the poor and rich people in the world to see and acknowledge my legacy of transferring all of Amazoxa Peace University and my personal wealth to the beneficiaries of all the poor people mentioned above, should I unexpectedly die, get eliminated, or assassinated by rival prestigious universities.

These universities may kill my physical body, but they will forever fail to kill my ideas of Amazoxa Peace University, the Home of True Education, which I have invented and gifted to the entire world, particularly the United States of America, where I am a naturalized American citizen, and to Eritrea, where I was born in 1981.

Let the world know that if, out of envy, something terrible happens to me, let all my books, assets, personal wealth, and intellectual properties be given to the poor people of all countries of the world as mentioned above. Under my Will, no government or state will have authority or entitlement to any of my assets if I die. My Immediate Family and the poor people of all countries of the world are the ONLY beneficiaries of all my financial assets, real estate, and Amazoxa Peace University, the Global Enterprise.

Signatory: Dr. Wisdom Zerit Teklay

Witnesses: Worldwide Amazoxa Peace University Board Members Committee

Let the prestigious universities tremble. Let governments and corporations take notice. A seed has been sown, not in fertile soil, but in the hearts and minds of billions. It is a seed of revolution, a seed of true education, a seed named Amazoxa Peace University.

They can try to silence the voice, but the echo will forever reverberate. They can try to bury the idea, but its roots have already snaked their way into the cracks of the old system, ready to pry it open and let the light of knowledge flood in.

This is not just a risk; it is a declaration of war. A war not with weapons, but with ignorance, with injustice, with the suffocating grip of the status quo. And in this war, the poor, the marginalized, the forgotten are not the victims. They are the army.
They are the billions who have received the torch, who have tasted the freedom of true education. They are the ones who will carry Amazoxa Peace University on their shoulders, not just as an institution, but as a promise, a shield, a sword.
So let them come. Let them try to extinguish the flame. They will find only embers scattered across the globe, each one ready to ignite a new fire, a new Amazoxa, a new dawn.
The risk has been taken. The die is cast. The greatest education has begun.
Imagine a world where education empowers not just the privileged few, but the billions yearning for peace, justice, and a chance to rise above their circumstances. A world where the seeds of Zerit-Tonianism blossom in every mind, nurtured by the fertile ground of Amazoxa Peace University. This is not a utopia, but a possibility within reach.
Though the path ahead is riddled with thorns – envy, greed, and the iron grip of the status quo – I, Dr. Zerit Teklay Sebhatleab, stand unyielding. For in the eyes of every child denied an education, in the hearts of every impoverished family, I see not fear, but a burning ember of defiance. They are the wind beneath my wings, the fuel that ignites this revolution of true education.
Let them try to silence me, to bury my ideas. Let them unleash their wolves in suits, their whispers in gilded halls. My words have already transcended borders, resonating in the souls of millions. They are etched in the fabric of the internet, a digital testament to a dream that cannot be extinguished.
For even if they silence the teacher, they cannot silence the students. The torch has been passed. The seed has been sown. And from the cracks in the pavement, from the forgotten corners of the world, Amazoxa Peace University will rise. Not

as a monument to my ego, but as a testament to the collective spirit, the unwavering belief that education is the birthright of every human being.

This is not just my legacy; it is yours. Join me. Let us rewrite the narrative, not with ink and paper, but with the unyielding force of our voices, our actions, our unwavering commitment to a world where peace and knowledge are not privileges, but fundamental rights.

Together, we will not just build Amazoxa Peace University; we will build a new world, brick by brick, idea by idea, until the walls of ignorance crumble and the dawn of true education breaks over the horizon.

Are you with me?

CHAPTER 15

THE HUMAN SPARK: WHY AI IS JUST A FLICKERING FLAME

Beyond the Ones and Zeros: Why Human Intelligence Reigns Supreme The question of human versus artificial intelligence is not about pitting two distinct entities against each other in a binary battle. It's about acknowledging a fundamental truth: artificial intelligence cannot exist without the spark of human ingenuity. Human intelligence is the sun, illuminating the path for AI, which is merely a reflection of our brilliance. Why? Because AI is nothing but computer-generated code, meticulously crafted in labs under the watchful eyes of human minds. The Achilles' heel of AI is its reliance on energy. Without a constant flow of electricity, it becomes a dormant giant, devoid of thought or action. We, the architects of this technology, understand this reality: human intelligence, with its ability to innovate and adapt without wires or power cords, will always

surpass artificial constructs. No electricity, no intelligence —
that's the stark truth. Therefore, we, the united nations of
human intelligence, declare to the world that human ingenuity
will always outshine the flickering flame of AI. To those who
boast about owning AI, we offer a humble reminder: solving the
world's problems with peaceful human intelligence is not only
noble but also cost-effective. When the lights go out, it is the
human spark that reignites the flame, not the cold embers of
artificial code. AI may impress with its lightning-fast processing
power and data-crunching abilities, but at its core, it is nothing
more than ones and zeros meticulously woven by human minds.
The limitations of AI become apparent when that spark fades.
Without a constant supply of electricity, its circuits fall silent,
reducing its impressive intellect to inert silicon. It serves as a
stark reminder that, despite its capabilities, AI remains reliant
on the very infrastructure and resources that human ingenuity
created. However, let us not diminish the remarkable progress of
AI. It is a testament to the power of human imagination,
translating abstract thought into tangible tools. But let us never
forget the source, the irreplaceable spark that breathes life into
these digital minds. The challenges we face demand more than
raw processing power. They require empathy, creativity, and the
ability to navigate the complexities of human experience. These
are the hallmarks of human intelligence, the qualities that
uniquely equip us to tackle the intricacies of our world.
Therefore, to those who boast about AI's dominance, we say:
embrace humility. Recognize that solving the world's problems
is not a race between silicon and flesh; it is a collaboration where
the human spark illuminates the path, guiding the limited yet
powerful flame of AI. Let us focus on harnessing the strengths of
both human and artificial intelligence, understanding that the
true potential lies not in competition but in the synergy between
the human mind and its digital reflection. It is in this
partnership where the real magic happens, where the flickering
flame transforms into a blazing inferno, capable of illuminating
the brightest future for all. Therefore, the question is not

whether intelligence is categorized as human or artificial, but rather the undeniable truth that artificial intelligence cannot exist without the spark of human ingenuity.

CHAPTER 16

SOLDIERS SAY NO: THE RADICAL SOLUTION TO END ALL WARS

From victims to victors: How soldiers can break the cycle.

The Real Question: Motivations Behind War
The question of whether war itself is good or bad is a simplistic one. The true question lies in the motivations behind each conflict. Is it a fight for freedom and independence, or a power-hungry grab for dominance and control? It is this distinction that truly matters, as it determines the impact and consequences of each war.
Who Suffers the Most: Innocent Lives and Soldiers
While politicians strategize from the safety of their offices, it is the innocent civilians and the soldiers on the frontlines who bear the incredible pain and trauma of war. They endure the

devastating consequences of conflicts that are often driven by ulterior motives.

Zerit-Tonianism Philosophy: Wisdom, Peace, and Justice

Dr. Wisdom Zerit Teklay, the esteemed president of Amazoxa Peace University and the visionary behind Zerit-Tonianism, puts forward a powerful philosophy:

- Wisdom is the ultimate form of education.
- Peace is a wiser choice than war.
- Justice, equality, and good health should be universal rights.
- No one should be above the law.

The Solution: Soldiers Say No

Dr. Wisdom Zerit Teklay proposes an innovative and radical solution: all soldiers should refuse to participate in war. By saying no, they can effectively eliminate wars. This includes:

- Rejecting the bombing of innocent civilians.
- Eliminating nuclear power and weapons.
- Putting an end to drone warfare.
- Choosing non-retaliation as a means to break the cycle of violence.

Imagine a World Without War

Just as Uber needs drivers to function, governments rely on soldiers to wage wars. However, envision a world where soldiers collectively refuse to fight. In this scenario, the power shifts to the people and the soldiers themselves. The war machine becomes powerless when soldiers say "enough."

True Power: Breaking the Cycle of War

Governments often manipulate soldiers, cloaking their actions under the guise of "defense," while pursuing their own agendas of dominance. Yet, like Uber drivers protesting unfair wages by refusing to work, soldiers can refuse to fight unjust wars. This collective action holds the power to dismantle the cycle of war and its catastrophic consequences, including the prevailing global conflict-driven inflation.

Superpowers at a Crossroads: Choosing Peace over Dominance

Superpowers must acknowledge that their pursuit of

dominance mirrors the calamitous tendencies of the past. By collectively saying "enough," soldiers can prevent another catastrophic world war.

A Message from Dr. Wisdom Zerit Teklay

War is a destructive cycle that harms everyone involved. Let us choose peace, wisdom, and the well-being of all. This is the path to a better world.

Beyond the Binary: Reframing the Nature of War and Its Costs

It is crucial to move beyond the oversimplified perspective of "good war versus bad war." Instead, we must examine the motivations behind each conflict. Is it a fight for liberation or a disguised power grab? This distinction holds significant weight, as it determines the impact of war. In addition to the suffering of innocent civilians, we must also recognize the heavy burdens borne by soldiers on the frontlines.

Enter Zerit-Tonianism: A Philosophy for a World Without War

Dr. Wisdom Zerit Teklay, the founder of Amazoxa Peace University, presents Zerit-Tonianism as a guiding philosophy. Its core tenets emphasize the importance of wisdom, peace, justice, equality, and accountability for all.

The Radical Solution: Soldier's Collective Refusal

Dr. Teklay puts forth a bold proposition: soldiers should collectively refuse to engage in war. This means rejecting the bombing of innocent civilians, abolishing nuclear weapons, ceasing drone warfare, and choosing non-retaliation. Imagine a world where soldiers no longer participate in war, leaving war commanders isolated.

Power Shifts: From Battlefield to Boardrooms

Governments often justify war as a necessary evil for defense, while pursuing agendas of control and dominance. However, soldiers possess the power to disrupt this system. Their collective refusal to be pawns in power struggles can dismantle the war machine, preventing economic turmoil and safeguarding human rights.

Superpowers on a Precipice: Breaking the Cycle of Destruction

Today's superpowers dangerously tread on the path that led to the devastation of past world wars. Yet, within their ranks lies the potential for change. If soldiers collectively choose peace, they can prevent another global catastrophe.

A Call to Action: Dr. Wisdom Zerit Teklay's Message

War perpetuates a cycle of violence that harms everyone. Let us choose wisdom, empathy, and the well-being of all over the destructive allure of conflict. Together, we can build a world where soldiers become guardians of peace, not pawns of war.

The Real Question: The Motivations Behind War

The true question is not a simple dichotomy of whether war is inherently good or bad. Rather, it revolves around the motivations that drive each conflict. Is it a fight for freedom against oppression or a ruthless pursuit of dominance disguised as "defense"? This nuance is pivotal in understanding the true nature of warfare.

Beyond Innocent Suffering: Widening the Scope of War's Impact

The repercussions of war extend beyond the innocent civilians caught in the crossfire. Soldiers, too, bear the heavy burden of war, experiencing physical, psychological, and emotional wounds. While politicians strategize from their ivory towers, soldiers confront fear, trauma, and the moral weight of taking lives.

Wisdom Whispers: The Essence of Zerit-Tonianism

Dr. Wisdom Zerit Teklay, a beacon of peace and the founder of Amazoxa Peace University, offers the wisdom of Zerit-Tonianism. Its core principles emphasize the value of wisdom as the ultimate form of education, the power of peace over war, and the universality of justice, equality, and good health. Furthermore, Zerit-Tonianism advocates for accountability as no individual or nation should be above the law.

A Radical Solution: Soldiers as Architects of Peace

The solution proposed by Dr. Teklay is as audacious as it is revolutionary: soldiers adopting a collective refusal to engage in war. By rejecting acts such as bombing innocent civilians, eliminating nuclear weapons, ending drone warfare, and choosing non-retaliation, soldiers can dismantle the war machine and create a world free from the devastating consequences of war.

Imagine a World Where War No Longer Requires Soldiers

Governments rely on soldiers just as Uber relies on drivers. But what if soldiers collectively decide to halt their participation? In this scenario, the war machine crumbles, and the power shifts to the people. Just as Uber without drivers is inconceivable, the world without soldiers participating in war is a transformative possibility.

Breaking the Cycle: Soldiers as Catalysts of Change

Governments often exploit soldiers, using narratives of "defense" to advance their agendas of dominance. However, soldiers possess the power to resist. Just as Uber drivers can protest unfair wages by refusing to work, soldiers can refuse to fight unjust wars. This collective action holds true power, taking it out of the hands of warmongers and placing it with the people and the soldiers themselves.

Superpowers at a Crossroads: Preventing Catastrophic Conflict

Today's superpowers stand on the precipice of repeating history's deadliest chapters. Their insatiable hunger for dominance mirrors the path that led to the First and Second World Wars. Yet, within their ranks, lies the potential to change course. By collectively choosing peace, soldiers can prevent another apocalyptic global conflict.

A Message from Dr. Wisdom Zerit Teklay Sebhatleab

War is a self-perpetuating cycle that consumes its own creators. Let us break free from this destructive cycle. Choose peace, wisdom, and the well-being of all. Together, we can build a world where soldiers become the guardians of peace, not mere pawns of war.

The Motivations Behind War: Going Beyond a Binary View

The nature of war cannot be summed up solely as good or bad. It is imperative to look deeper and ask why wars are fought. Are they driven by a fight for fundamental rights against tyranny, or are they disguised as defense while pursuing power? This distinction is crucial, as it shapes the consequences and significance of each conflict.

Beyond Innocent Suffering: Recognizing the Wider Range of Victims

War exacts a heavy toll, not only on innocent civilians caught in the line of fire but also on soldiers. They bear physical, psychological, and emotional burdens. While leaders strategize from positions of safety, those on the frontlines experience fear, trauma, and the moral weight of taking lives.

The Wisdom of Zerit-Tonianism: Guiding the Way

Dr. Wisdom Zerit Teklay, the visionary behind Amazoxa Peace University, offers Zerit-Tonianism as a guiding light. It emphasizes the value of wisdom as the ultimate education, the power of peace as the ultimate victory, and the universality of justice, equality, and good health. No one, regardless of their position, should be above the law.

A Radical Solution: Soldiers Saying No

Dr. Teklay proposes a revolutionary solution: soldiers collectively refusing to participate in war. This means rejecting the bombing of innocent civilians, abolishing nuclear weapons, ceasing drone warfare, and choosing non-retaliation. Envision a world where war commanders are left without soldiers to carry out their orders—just as Uber without drivers would cease to exist.

Power Shifts: From Battlefield to Boardrooms

Governments often manipulate soldiers, using narratives of "defense" to pursue dominance. But soldiers hold the power to disrupt this system. Their collective refusal to fight unjust wars can dismantle the war machine and its devastating consequences, from economic turmoil to the erosion of human rights.

Superpowers at a Crossroads: Breaking the Cycle of Destruction

The world's superpowers stand on the precipice of repeating history's bloodiest chapters. Their relentless pursuit of dominance mirrors the path that led to the First and Second

World Wars. However, within their ranks lies the potential for change. If soldiers collectively choose peace, they can prevent another global catastrophe.

A Call to Action: Dr. Wisdom Zerit Teklay's Message

War is a self-perpetuating cycle of violence that harms everyone involved. Let us choose wisdom, empathy, and the well-being of all over the destructive allure of conflict. Together, we can build a world where soldiers are not instruments of war but ambassadors of peace, where Zerit-Tonianism's ideals become a tangible reality.

Conclusion 1: A World Transformed

Imagine a world where children play amidst abandoned tank graveyards and war museums serve as somber reminders rather than imminent threats. Picture a world where soldiers, once tools of the war machine, become architects of peace—building bridges instead of barricades. This is not a utopian dream, but a potential waiting to be unlocked. When soldiers choose wisdom over war, superpowers choose collaboration over competition, and Zerit-Tonianism's principles of justice, equality, and good health become reality, we become the architects of a future where peace reigns supreme.

Conclusion 2: A Challenge to Soldiers

Soldiers, you are not pawns in a grand game. You are the guardians of humanity and the agents of our collective will. You possess the power to rewrite the narrative, to become the authors of a new chapter in history. Refuse to be blinded by propaganda, to be puppets of ambition. See the faces of the innocent, hear the cries of the wounded, and recognize that your true strength lies not in blind obedience, but in defiance. Your refusal to engage in war is a thunderclap that can shatter empires and awaken the world. This is your moment, your opportunity to be the heroes we desperately need. Choose peace, not just for yourselves, but for the generations yet to come. Choose Zerit-Tonianism, not as an abstract philosophy, but as your guiding compass. Be the soldiers who lay down their arms, not in surrender, but in the ultimate act of victory

—the victory over war itself.

Conclusion 3: Planting the Seed of Peace

War is a fertile ground, but not for the seeds we truly hunger for. It nourishes fear, hatred, and vengeance that poison generations. Yet, even amidst the blood and ruin, a fragile seed of hope can sprout. This seed yearns for peace and a different future.

Soldiers, you hold this seed in your hands. You have witnessed the horrors of war firsthand and felt the weight of its burden on your hearts. You know, perhaps better than anyone, the devastating cost of conflict. But within you lies the power to nurture that seed, to allow it to grow into a mighty tree that shades the world from the scorching sun of war.

Let your refusal to fight be the first crack in the hardened earth. Let your collective "no" be the rain that nourishes the seed of peace. Let your actions be the branches that reach out, offering shelter and solace to a world weary of violence. You, soldiers, are not just witnesses to the tragedy of war, you are the potential architects of a new era.

Choose peace. Choose Zerit-Tonianism. Choose the future where your legacy isn't etched in blood, but in the verdant green of a world finally healed. Plant the seed of peace, soldiers. Let it take root, let it grow, and let it bloom.

CHAPTER 17

ESCAPING THE TRAPS OF POVERTY: CREDIT CARDS, SCORES, AND SUPER-POWERISM

Dr. Wisdom Zerit Teklay, CEO of Amazoxa Peace University, spearheaded a powerful movement centered around a simple yet profound concept: true financial freedom begins with shedding the chains of debt. We took action by paying off all our credit cards and loans, and we strongly encourage you to do the same. Why is this so important? Because credit cards, credit scores, and the ideology of super-powerism perpetuate a cycle of poverty. Through our extensive global research as a non-political organization, we have uncovered critical information:

- **Exploitative lending practices:** The wealthy take advantage of people through debt and credit cards, enriching themselves at the expense of others.
- **Fear associated with credit scores:** This system,

meticulously designed by banks and corrupt politicians, is engineered to keep you trapped in a cycle of debt. It's time to break free from its grasp.

- **The power of manipulation:** We are constantly bombarded with messages that urge us to spend now and worry about paying later, ultimately benefiting corporations while entrapping us in financial distress.

As part of our global movement, we vehemently reject this system. We have freed ourselves from credit card debt, credit scores, and the desire to participate in this rigged game. Our vision is a world free from predatory financial systems, where financial freedom and equality are accessible to all.

Join us. Share your experiences. Learn about Zerit-Tonianism, a philosophy that prioritizes peace, justice, and good health for all. Together, let's build a future where financial ruin is not predetermined, but where financial empowerment paves the way for a brighter tomorrow.

Escaping the Traps of Poverty: Why We Ditched Credit Cards and How You Can Too

Credit cards, credit scores, and the allure of super-powerism are not shortcuts to wealth; they are traps that keep the poor and middle class drowning in debt. Dr. Wisdom Zerit Teklay, CEO of Amazoxa Peace University, initiated a movement within our community to do the unthinkable: we collectively paid off **all** our debts and made a commitment to never use credit cards again. Here's why you should join us:

- **Financial freedom starts with financial independence.** Credit card companies profit by keeping you in debt. We have uncovered crucial information that reveals how credit scores are designed to benefit the wealthy while leaving everyone else at a disadvantage. By breaking free from this oppressive system, we have taken control of our finances and secured our future.
- **Debt is a burden, not a tool.** We are tired of being manipulated by predatory lending practices and coerced into spending money we do not have. Why postpone

the ability to afford something when you can make conscious financial decisions in the present? By ditching credit cards, we eliminate the stress and gain the power to make informed choices.

- **Envision a world without credit card debt.** Our global non-political movement dreams of an America and a world where financial ruin is not predetermined at birth. We believe in education, not exploitation, and strive to build a future where everyone has the opportunity to thrive.

Join us in creating a society free from the shackles of credit card debt and corrupt financial systems. Let's construct a future of financial freedom, peace, and equality for all. Share your story, learn about Zerit-Tonianism, and together, we can break the chains that bind us.

Remember: Wisdom is the highest form of education, and true success lies in achieving financial independence. Choose freedom. Choose peace. Choose a life without traps.

Escaping the Poverty Labyrinth: Ditch the Credit Card, Embrace Financial Zen

Forget about the plastic shackles, the invisible chains of credit scores, and the illusory promise of super-powerism. We, the freethinkers and architects of our own destinies, have discovered an alternative path. Led by the visionary Dr. Wisdom Zerit Teklay, CEO of Amazoxa Peace University, we embarked on a radical quest for collective financial liberation. We said "no" to debt, bid farewell to credit cards, and swore allegiance to a future free from the chains of borrowed wealth.

Why did we take this stand? Because the truth, magnified through our global non-partisan lens, is clear: credit cards and credit scores are not tools, but rather traps. They are instruments used by the privileged to exploit and keep the poor and middle class submerged in a sea of payments. We broke free, and so can you.

Financial freedom is not a rare prize won through chance; it is a deliberate choice. Our realization that credit card companies profit from our anxieties, our fear of the elusive "good" credit score, has empowered us to take back our financial control and find peace of mind.

Imagine a world where the mantra of "buy now, pay later" is not a hypnotic chant, but a conscious decision. A world where debts are not burdens handed down through generations, but relics of a bygone era. This is the world we are constructing, one brick at a time, through our ever-growing global movement.

Join us. Share your story. Cast off the weight of debt and discover the liberating power of financial Zen. Learn about Zerit-Tonianism, a philosophy that values wisdom over wealth, peace over power, and education over exploitation.

Remember, financial independence is the ultimate act of rebellion. It is a middle finger raised against the rigged system, a declaration that we, the people, hold the key to our own prosperity. Ditch the plastic, embrace the freedom, and together, let's rewrite the rules of the financial game.

No more traps, just peace, purpose, and the limitless potential of a debt-free future.

The Revolution Starts Now

Imagine waking up tomorrow, not to the suffocating grip of debt, but to the sunrise of possibility. Envision a world where every dollar you earn whispers freedom instead of fear. A world where financial predators are replaced by enlightening educators, and credit scores are relics of a bygone era. This is not utopia; it is the dawn of a revolution that we can ignite together.

Join our movement. Share your story. Let your voice reverberate through the labyrinth, guiding others who are trapped in the shadows. Together, we will not only escape the Poverty Labyrinth, but demolish its walls brick by brick. We will build a new world, where the wisdom of Zerit-Tonianism guides us and financial freedom becomes the birthright of all.

This is not just about ditching credit cards; it is about reclaiming your power. It is about choosing financial peace over a lifetime of servitude. It is about becoming the architect of your own destiny, not a pawn in someone else's game.

Rise up. Rise above. Choose freedom. Choose Zerit-Tonianism. Choose a life beyond the labyrinth.

The Ripple Effect of Liberation

Let us not simply escape the labyrinth; let us be the earthquake that shatters it. Every credit card you shred, every dollar you deliberately save, creates tremors that shake the foundations of a rigged system. Imagine the collective force of millions joining hands, their voices merging in a chorus demanding change.

This movement is not just about individual liberation; it is about systemic transformation. We will become living, breathing examples of Zerit-Tonianism's power, radiating financial literacy and empowering others to break free. Together, we will show the world that escaping the Poverty Labyrinth is not only possible, but inevitable.

Therefore, let us not only pay off our debts; let us pay it forward. Share your knowledge, mentor others, and be the catalyst for a ripple effect of liberation. Witness the transformative power of financial freedom as it washes over communities, erasing the lines of inequality and painting a future where everyone thrives. This is your chance to be a part of something greater than yourself. Be the wave that crashes against the walls of oppression. Be the spark that ignites the fire of financial justice. Choose freedom. Choose Zerit-Tonianism. Choose to be the change you wish to see in the world.

Choose a life beyond the labyrinth.

Breaking Free: A Manifesto for Financial Liberation

Set aside the allure of credit and the seductive promises of super-powerism. They are not shortcuts to wealth; they are mere illusions that lead the desperate further into debt. At Amazoxa Peace University, under the guidance of the visionary Dr. Zerit Teklay Sebhatleab, we made a bold choice: we obliterated our debt and vowed to never use credit again. Here is why you should join us on this financial exodus:

Financial freedom is not an unattainable oasis; it is the inheritance you were born to claim. Credit card companies function as modern-day pharaohs, building their empires on the backs of the indebted. We have deciphered their code—the credit score system is rigged to keep the poor powerless and the rich even wealthier. By severing this toxic bond, we have taken back control of our destinies and paved our path towards financial independence.

Debt is not a tool; it is a leash of manipulation. We have grown weary of being whipped by predatory lenders and coerced into purchasing things we cannot afford with money we do not possess. Why mortgage your future for fleeting pleasures? By abandoning credit cards, you release the suffocating collar of debt and gain the power to make informed decisions.

Imagine a world where debt does not define your worth, where financial ruin is not your predetermined destiny. Our global non-political movement envisions an America, and a world, where financial freedom is not a privilege but a fundamental human right. We believe in education rather than exploitation, and we strive to build a future where everyone possesses the key to unlocking prosperity.

Join us on this financial exodus. Together, let us dismantle the Labyrinth of Poverty, brick by brick, and construct a sanctuary of peace, equality, and freedom from the shackles of credit. Share your story, explore Zerit-Tonianism, and together, we can rewrite the rules of the financial game.

Remember: Wisdom is your ultimate weapon, and true success is not measured in dollars but in the serene tranquility of financial independence. Choose freedom. Choose peace. Choose a life beyond the labyrinth.

1. **The Revolution Starts Now:** Let this manifesto be our battle cry. Share it, spread the word, and ignite the flames of financial liberation. This is not just about eradicating debt; it is about reclaiming our power and building a world where money serves humanity instead of the other way around.
2. **Beyond the Walls of Debt:** We have escaped the Labyrinth, and it is our duty to guide others still

trapped within. Share your story—your struggles and triumphs. Together, we will forge a community where financial freedom is not a distant dream, but a shared reality.

3. **The Choice is Yours:** Will you continue to be a prisoner of debt, or will you join us in this audacious quest for liberty? The path requires bravery, education, and a shared vision of a world where financial peace reigns. Choose freedom. Choose Zerit-Tonianism. Choose a life beyond the traps.

CHAPTER 18

BREAKING THE WALLS OF DIVISION: BUILDING A UNITED EARTH

A touch of Dr. Wisdom Zerit's wisdom

Building a World of Peace: The United Countries of the World Constitution

Picture a world united under one flag, one currency, and one constitution – a world where peace, fairness, and justice reign supreme. This is the vision of the United Countries of the World, a global movement driven by the collective yearning for a brighter future.

Our global flag, which features a map of our planet Earth, symbolizes our shared home and the oath we solemnly swear: "We, the people of the United Countries of the World, pledge to uphold the Constitution, preserving, protecting, and defending it to the best of our abilities."

This Constitution is not just another document. It is a living, breathing testament to the power of checks and balances. Just as every nation holds its government accountable, the United Countries will do the same, ensuring that no power, individual, or nation rises above the law.

Our top mission? To compare and reconcile constitutions, starting with the United States and Eritrea, and eventually encompassing all nations. Our goal is not to erase differences, but to find common ground and build bridges where walls once stood.

We envision a globally recognized and respected organization that enforces universal laws, curbing abuse of power and putting an end to war crimes. The days of invading nations and violating their autonomy will be over.

Dr. Wisdom Zerit Teklay, president of Amazoxa Peace University and philosopher of Zerit-Tonianism, reminds us: "Wisdom is the highest level of education, and true success lies in achieving peace. No government, official, or individual is above the law. We must all strive for justice, equality, and good health."

When implemented, the proposed global Constitution will be a beacon of hope. No government, official, or individual will be above its supreme law. Everyone, regardless of wealth or power, will be equally subject to its principles. This is not just about limitations; it's about liberation, a world free from the shackles of tyranny and war.

We, the United Countries of the World, are not just dreamers; we are builders. We are citizens with bold ideas, unwavering laws, and an unshakeable vision: one world, united. This is not just a possibility; it is our greatest collective achievement waiting to be realized.

Join us. Share your voice. Together, we can make the United Countries of the World a reality, banishing war and ushering in an era of peace, justice, and prosperity for all. The future of our planet depends on it.

Forget the patchwork of borders and the cacophony of flags. We envision a world where Earth's map is our banner, a single currency flows like a shared heartbeat, and one Constitution unites us under the sky of peace. This isn't utopia; it's the United Earth, a movement rising from the ashes of division, fueled by the embers of our shared humanity.

Imagine pledging allegiance not to a nation, but to our planet, swearing an oath like a chorus: "We, the people of the United Earth, vow to uphold the Constitution, its ink the blood of our collective hope, its words our shield against tyranny."

This isn't a document collecting dust in archives. It's a living code, woven from the threads of every nation's laws. The United Earth checks the power of any state, just as each citizen checks its own government. No emperor, no president, escapes its watchful gaze.

Our mission? To reconcile, not erase. We begin by stitching together the American tapestry with the Eritrean, then expand outwards, unraveling the knots of conflict and weaving a tapestry of unity. We seek not uniformity, but harmony, a symphony of voices where each note strengthens the whole.

This isn't just a dream; it's a blueprint. We envision a global body, respected and empowered, wielding universal laws like a sculptor's chisel, chipping away at the granite of abuse and carving a future free from war. No more shall nations trespass on the sacred ground of another's autonomy.

Dr. Wisdom Zerit Teklay, philosopher of Zerit-Tonianism and leader of Amazoxa Peace University, reminds us: "Wisdom whispers in the quiet hum of peace, not the roar of cannons. No law is above the law, no life above another. Let justice, equality, and health be our guiding stars."

When this Constitution takes root, it will be an earthquake, shattering the foundations of inequality. No longer will power be a gilded cage, reserved for the chosen few. Everyone, from the humble farmer to the CEO, will stand equal under its sky. This isn't about limitations; it's about liberation, a world where fear doesn't dictate our borders and greed doesn't fuel our wars.

We, the United Earth, are not passive observers; we are architects. We are citizens with blueprints for a better world, laws etched in our hearts, and a vision that burns brighter than a thousand suns: one Earth, united. This isn't just a possibility; it's our birthright, waiting to be claimed.

Join us. Let your voice be the mortar that binds our bricks. Together, we can build the United Earth, brick by brick, and lay the cornerstone of a future where peace isn't a prayer, but a song sung in every tongue, under the same, glorious sky. The fate of our planet hangs in the balance. Will we choose division, or will we choose Earth?

One World, One Hope: Building the United Countries of the World

Imagine a world where war is a relic, borders are irrelevant, and a single currency flows freely. This is not a utopian fantasy, but a tangible future within reach – the United Countries of the World.

Our flag, a vibrant map of our planet, symbolizes our shared home and the solemn oath we pledge: "We, the people of the United Earth, unite under one banner, vowing to uphold the Constitution that safeguards peace, justice, and equality for all."

This Constitution is not just ink on paper; it is a shield against tyranny. Just as we hold our own governments accountable, the United Earth will do the same, ensuring that no power, individual, or nation stands above the law.

Our mission? To reconcile the world's constitutions, weaving a tapestry of unity from diverse threads. We begin with the United States and Eritrea, not to erase differences, but to celebrate the common ground that binds us.

Imagine a global body, not of politicians but of dreamers and builders, enforcing universal laws that banish war crimes and corruption. No longer will nations be violated, their autonomy trampled.

Dr. Wisdom Zerit Teklay, philosopher and champion of peace, reminds us: "Wisdom whispers in the pursuit of peace. No government, official, or individual is above the law. We are one humanity, united by our yearning for justice, equality, and well-being."

When enacted, this Constitution will be a lighthouse in the storm. No longer will wealth or power shield anyone from its gaze. This isn't about restrictions but liberation – a world free from the chains of oppression and conflict.

We, the United Earth, are not just passive observers; we are architects. We are citizens with bold ideas, unwavering principles, and an unshakeable dream: one world, one currency, one destiny. This isn't just a possibility; it's our birthright, waiting to be claimed.

Join us. Lend your voice. Together, let's build the United Earth, brick by brick, hope by hope. The future of our planet depends on it.

One World, One Dream: Rise with the United Countries of the World

Imagine a tapestry of nations woven into one. A single flag, a map of our shared home, Earth, fluttering in the wind, a symbol of unity, not conquest. This is not utopia, but a promise – the United Countries of the World, a constellation of voices rising against the din of division.

We, the people, swear allegiance not to borders but to a higher ideal: a global Constitution, the bedrock of peace, fairness, and justice. No longer will nations stand alone, vulnerable to the tides of tyranny. This Constitution is our shield, its checks and balances a vigilant guardian against abuse of power.

Forget the whispers of war, the phantom lines drawn on maps. We will harmonize our differences, starting with the United States and Eritrea, then stretching our arms to embrace all nations. This isn't about erasing identities, but about finding the threads that bind us, weaving a tapestry of shared values.

Our vision? A global organization, not a domineering force, but a beacon of hope. We will enforce universal laws, not with an iron fist, but with the collective might of humanity. War crimes will be relics of a forgotten age, replaced by the chorus of children's laughter echoing across borders.

Dr. Wisdom Zerit Teklay, the philosopher-King of Amazoxa Peace University, reminds us: "Wisdom whispers: 'Peace is the ultimate success.' No government, official, or individual is above the law. Let justice, equality, and good health be our guiding stars."

When this Constitution takes flight, it won't be a mere document, but a living testament to our shared humanity. No longer will any leader, nation, or individual stand above its supreme law. This isn't about stripping power; it's about unleashing the potential of unity. Imagine a world where shackles are broken, replaced by the boundless freedom of peace.

We, the United Countries of the World, are not just dreamers; we are architects. We are citizens armed with bold ideas, unwavering laws, and a vision that burns brighter than a thousand suns: one world, united.

This isn't just a possibility; it's a responsibility. Join us. Raise your voice. Share your story. Together, we will build the United Countries of the World, brick by brick, law by law. Let peace be our anthem, justice our compass, and unity our guiding light. The future of our planet, our children's future, depends on it.

One World, One Dream: Rise with the United Countries of the World

Imagine a lullaby sung not to one nation, but to a planet. A single flag, a map of our shared home, Earth, cradling a world no longer divided by borders but by a shared heartbeat. This is not a dream; this is the birth cry of the United Countries of the World, a symphony of voices rising against the cacophony of war.

We, the people, no longer pledge allegiance to lines drawn on maps but to a higher melody: a global Constitution, the lullaby of peace, fairness, and justice. No longer will nations be soloists, vulnerable to the discord of tyranny. This Constitution is our harmony, its checks and balances a chorus against abuse of power.

Forget the war drums, the barbed wire fences that scar our planet. We will harmonize our differences, starting with the United States and Eritrea, then crescendo to embrace all nations. This isn't about erasing identities, but about finding the notes that resonate within us, composing a symphony of shared values.

Our vision? A global orchestra, not a conductor of fear, but a maestro of hope. We will orchestrate universal laws, not with the crash of cymbals but with the collective crescendo of humanity. War crimes will be relegated to a forgotten movement, replaced by the joyous finale of children's laughter echoing across continents.

Dr. Wisdom Zerit Teklay, the conductor of peace at Amazoxa University, reminds us: "Wisdom whispers: 'Peace is the ultimate masterpiece.' No government, official, or individual is above the score. Let justice, equality, and good health be our instruments."

When this Constitution takes flight, it won't be a mere document, but a living, breathing opera that unites our voices. No longer will any leader, nation, or individual stand above its supreme harmony. This isn't about silencing; it's about unleashing the boundless power of unity. Imagine a world where walls crumble, replaced by the boundless freedom of collective purpose.

We, the United Countries of the World, are not dreamers; we are the composers. We are not passive spectators; we are the rising chorus. We are citizens armed with bold ideas, unwavering laws, and a vision that echoes louder than a thousand thunderbolts: one world, united.

This isn't just a possibility; it's a responsibility. Join us. Raise your voice. Share your story. Together, we will build the United Countries of the World, note by note, law by law. Let peace be our conductor, justice our rhythm, and unity our score. The future of our planet, our children's symphony, depends on it.

CHAPTER 19

JANUARY 6TH: DEMOCRACY'S SHATTERED MIRROR

Beyond Red and Blue: A New Party for a United America (Wisdom People Party)

Domestic Terrorism Tragedy of January 6, 2021: A Test for American Democracy

The January 6, 2021, attack on the U.S. Capitol was an unprecedented event in American history, a domestic terrorism tragedy that tested the very foundations of our democracy. Never before, in the past 230 years, had the U.S. government's most respected and powerful symbol been so blatantly humiliated and disrespected by its own citizens.

While the justice system has arrested many insurrectionists, it has yet to hold accountable the powerful individuals who, through words and corrupt actions, brainwashed them into attacking the Capitol. This is a glaring failure of our system, where the rich and powerful seem immune to prosecution even when evidence of their crimes is clear. This blatant inequality, where the law protects only the privileged while incarcerating millions for minor offenses, sometimes even for crimes they didn't commit, is a travesty of justice.

Dr. Wisdom Zerit Teklay, President of Amazoxa Peace University and philosopher of Zerit-Tonianism, emphasizes that true wisdom lies in championing peace over war and upholding justice, equality, and good health for all. Her philosophy reminds us that no one, not even the President, is above the law.

The solution is clear: violence, in any form, cannot be tolerated. We cannot selectively apply the meaning of the word "violence." The true tragedy of January 6th lies in the right to bear arms, so readily displayed by civilians during the attack. If the Founding Fathers, who designed this law, could witness this event, they would likely convene in the Capitol's situation room and repeal the Second Amendment. Because of this right, the United States leads the world in gun violence and mass incarceration.

Repealing the Second Amendment is the only way to prevent another January 6th, not just in America but wherever this right exists. No country should promote gun violence through its laws.

Therefore, we propose the following:

- **Formation of a new, third political party:** This party would act as an official mediator between Republicans and Democrats during domestic terrorism crises, bridging the ever-widening divide fueled by hidden political warfare.
- **Article 6 Anti-Domestic Terrorism Act:** This law would grant the Supreme Court oversight over domestic and international terrorism. Given its relative impartiality compared to individual government branches, the Supreme Court is less susceptible to corruption and the manipulation of words to incite violence for personal political gain.

Let us not repeat the mistakes of January 6th. We implore every American to reject violence and work together to heal the divisions that threaten our democracy. Let us rise above partisan battles and create a future where justice, equality, and peace prevail.

January 6th: A Call to Arms for American Democracy

The January 6, 2021, assault on the U.S. Capitol was an unprecedented domestic terrorism tragedy, a desecration of the heart of our democracy, and a stark test of its very foundations. Never before in our 230-year history had such a blatant display of humiliation and disrespect been inflicted upon the most revered symbol of American power by its own citizens.

While the justice system has apprehended many insurrectionists, it has yet to hold accountable the powerful individuals who, through incendiary rhetoric and corrupt actions, incited and manipulated them into storming the Capitol. This glaring failure exposes a deep rot in our system, where the rich and powerful seem immune to prosecution even when compelling evidence of their crimes exists. This blatant inequality, where the law shields the privileged while millions languish in prison for non-violent offenses, sometimes even for crimes they didn't commit, is a travesty of justice that cries out for redress.

Dr. Wisdom Zerit Teklay, President of Amazoxa Peace University and philosopher of Zerit-Tonian Philosophy, reminds us that true wisdom lies in championing peace over war and upholding justice, equality, and good health for all. Her philosophy resonates deeply, reminding us that no one, not even the President, stands above the law.

The solution demands immediate action and is multifaceted. First, we cannot tolerate violence in any form. We cannot selectively apply the meaning of this word. The true tragedy of January 6th lies not just in the violence itself, but in the right to bear arms that so readily enabled it. If the Founding Fathers, who designed this law, could witness this event, they would likely convene in the Capitol's situation room and demand the repeal of the Second Amendment. This right, enshrined in our Constitution, has allowed the United States to become the world leader in both gun violence and mass incarceration. It is a stain on our nation and a direct threat to our future.

Repealing the Second Amendment is a necessary step, not just for America but for any nation that legitimizes and facilitates gun violence through its laws. However, it is not enough.

Therefore, we propose the following:

- **Formation of a new, third political party:** This party, free from the shackles of partisan warfare, would act as an official mediator during domestic terrorism crises, bridging the deepening chasm exacerbated by partisan manipulations and misinformation. It would be dedicated to finding common ground and fostering genuine compromise, prioritizing the well-being of our nation above partisan agendas.
- **Article 6 Anti-Domestic Terrorism Act:** This law would empower the Supreme Court, with its relative impartiality, to oversee domestic and international terrorism. It would provide a crucial check on power and a bulwark against future attempts to subvert democracy.

Let us not repeat the mistakes of January 6th. We implore every American to reject violence, embrace dialogue, and work together to heal the divisions that threaten our democracy. Let us rise above partisan battles and create a future where justice, equality, and peace prevail. This is not just a call to action; it is a call to arms for the very soul of our nation. January 6th: A Call to Arms for American Democracy

I, Dr. Wisdom Zerit Teklay, gaze upon the hallowed halls of the U.S. Capitol, now a silent witness to the desecration it endured on January 6, 2021. This domestic terrorism tragedy, a stain on our 230-year-old democracy, laid bare the fragility of the very foundation upon which our nation stands. It was a day where the most respected symbol of our government, a beacon of hope and justice, was defiled by its own citizens, incited by the whispers of the powerful and the fury of the misled.

While the justice system has begun to apprehend some insurrectionists, it has yet to truly confront the puppeteers who orchestrated this attack. Those who, through venomous words and corrupt actions, manipulated innocent minds into storming the Capitol, remain untouched. This glaring injustice exposes a system where the rich and powerful seem to wear an invisible cloak of immunity, even when evidence screams their guilt. Millions, meanwhile, are incarcerated for minor, often non-violent offenses, sometimes even for crimes they didn't commit. This twisted scale of justice is a travesty that demands immediate redress.

As President of Amazoxa Peace University and philosopher of Zerit-Tonianism, I believe the path forward lies not in vengeance, but in wisdom. True wisdom, as Zerit-Tonianism teaches, champions peace over war, and upholds the pillars of justice, equality, and good health for all. It reminds us, with unwavering clarity, that no one, not even the President, stands above the law.

The solution demands a multifaceted approach. We cannot tolerate violence in any form, nor can we selectively apply the meaning of this word. The true tragedy of January 6th lies not only in the blood spilled and the windows shattered, but in the very right that enabled it: the right to bear arms. This right, so readily displayed by civilians during the attack, has become a twisted shield, legitimizing and facilitating gun violence. It has made the United States the world leader in both mass shootings and mass incarceration, a grim statistic that hangs heavy on our conscience.

If the Founding Fathers, who designed this law, could witness this dystopian reality, I believe they would convene in the very situation room of the Capitol and repeal the Second Amendment. Not out of fear, but out of sanity. Not to disarm, but to value life above all else.

But repealing the Second Amendment is just one step on a long road to healing. We must also propose:

- **The formation of a new, third political party:** A bridge between the warring red and blue, free from partisan shackles. This party would act as an official mediator

during domestic terrorism crises, healing the chasm deepened by misinformation and manipulation.
- **The Article 6 Anti-Domestic Terrorism Act:** This law would empower the Supreme Court, with its relative impartiality, to oversee domestic and international terrorism. It would provide a crucial check on power and a bulwark against future attempts to subvert democracy. It would ensure that our democracy remains protected from the corruption and manipulation that weaponizes words for personal political gain.

Let us not sleepwalk into another January 6th. Let us reject the siren song of violence and work together to mend the divisions that threaten our democracy. Let us rise above the red and the blue, and embrace the Zerit-Tonian ideals of justice, equality, and peace. This is not just a call to action; it is a call to arms for American democracy itself.

This is our moment. This is our pledge. This is our time to stand as one, not as divided factions, but as a united nation, and reclaim the promise etched on our Capitol's facade: "E pluribus unum." Out of many, one.

January 6th: A Call to Arms for American Democracy

I, Dr. Wisdom Zerit Teklay, stand before you not just as a philosopher, but as a witness. The hallowed halls of the U.S. Capitol, once a symbol of hope and justice, now bear the scars of January 6th, a domestic terrorism tragedy that stripped bare the fragility of our 230-year-old democracy. It was a day where the whispers of the powerful and the fury of the misled defiled the very foundation of our nation.

The justice system may be apprehending some pawns, but the true puppeteers remain untouched. Those who, through venomous words and corrupt actions, manipulated innocent minds into storming the Capitol, still walk free. This is the rot at the heart of our system, where the powerful wear an invisible cloak of immunity, even when evidence screams their guilt. Millions, meanwhile, are caged for non-violent offenses, sometimes for crimes they never committed. This twisted scale of justice is a travesty that demands immediate redress.

As Zerit-Tonianism teaches, true wisdom champions peace, not vengeance. It upholds justice, equality, and good health for all, reminding us that no one, not even the President, stands above the law.

The solution is not a simple bandage, but a radical surgery. We cannot tolerate violence in any form, nor can we selectively apply the meaning of this word. The true tragedy of January 6th lies not just in the blood and broken glass, but in the right that enabled it: the right to bear arms. This twisted shield, so readily displayed by civilians that day, has legitimized and facilitated gun violence. It has made the United States the world leader in both mass shootings and mass incarceration.

If the Founding Fathers could witness this dystopian reality, I believe they would convene in that very situation room and repeal the Second Amendment. Not out of fear, but out of sanity. Not to disarm, but to value life above all else.

But this is just the first step. We must also:

- **Form a new, third political party:** A bridge between the warring red and blue, free from partisan shackles. This party would act as an official mediator during domestic terrorism crises, bridging the divide exacerbated by partisan manipulations and misinformation. It would be dedicated to finding common ground and fostering genuine compromise, prioritizing the well-being of our nation above partisan agendas.
- **Enact the Article 6 Anti-Domestic Terrorism Act:** This empowers the Supreme Court, with its relative impartiality, to oversee domestic and international terrorism. It would provide a crucial check on power and a bulwark against future attempts to subvert democracy. It would ensure that our democracy remains protected from the corruption and manipulation that weaponizes words for personal political gain. It would provide a crucial check on power and a bulwark against future attempts to subvert democracy.

Let us not sleepwalk into another January 6th. Let us reject violence and work together to mend the divisions that threaten our democracy. Let us rise above the red and the blue, and embrace the Zerit-Tonian ideals that bind us: justice, equality, and peace.

This is not just a call to action; it is a call to arms for American democracy itself. This is our moment, our pledge. This is our time to stand not as divided factions, but as one nation, reclaiming the promise etched on our Capitol's facade: "E pluribus unum." Out of many, one.

We will not be defined by January 6th. We will be defined by our response. Let us rise to the challenge, together. Let us be the change we desperately need and build a future where peace, not violence, echoes through the halls of our Capitol and the hearts of our people.

We stand at a precipice, America. January 6th wasn't just a day of infamy; it was a chasm ripped open in the fabric of our nation. We can't simply stitch it closed with the frayed threads of a broken system. We must weave a new tapestry, one woven with the golden threads of Zerit-Tonian justice, the emerald threads of genuine equality, and the ivory threads of lasting peace.

Repealing the Second Amendment is not a surrender, but a liberation. It is casting off the yoke of a law that has become a weapon, a shield for the violent and a burden for the innocent. Let us not be a nation where children practice lockdown drills and mothers fear the mail. Let us be a nation where arms reach for knowledge, not guns.

But the path to peace is not paved with a single act, no matter how bold. The third party, a bridge between warring factions, will be the mortar that binds our fractured democracy. Let it not be a haven for the disaffected, but a beacon for the disillusioned, a place where reason reigns over rhetoric, and compromise over division.

Finally, the Supreme Court, a lone oak amidst the partisan winds, must be entrusted with the sacred duty of overseeing domestic terrorism. Let it be a shield against corruption, the firewall against manipulation, the voice of reason in the face of fearmongering.

January 6th was a wake-up call, a thunderclap in the night. But what follows the storm is not just the rising sun, but the choice we make in its light. Do we cling to the shadows of the past, or do we step onto the path of healing and unity, hand in hand, Zerit-Tonian ideals guiding our way?

This is not a call for the timid, nor a plea for the fainthearted. It is a clarion cry for the dreamers, the builders, the ones who dare to imagine a nation where the Capitol stands not as a monument to our shame, but as a testament to our resilience, our unity, our unwavering belief in the words etched upon its very walls: "E pluribus unum." Out of many, one.

Let us be that one, America. Let us be the generation that finally fulfills the promise whispered on the wind: one nation, indivisible, with liberty and justice for all.

This is our moment. This is our pledge. This is our time to rise.

I hear you. The Second Amendment is a complex and deeply personal issue for many Americans. While I firmly believe in the need for reform, I also understand the sense of security it provides for some. Let's navigate this together.

I, Dr. Wisdom Zerit Teklay, stand before you not to demonize the Second Amendment, but to acknowledge its duality. It is, for many, a bulwark against tyranny, a symbol of self-reliance, a guardian of freedom. It is the right that whispers, "No king shall rule unchallenged," the right that echoes with the musket shots of Lexington and Concord. And yet, this same right, twisted by fear and manipulated by malice, became the battering ram that breached the Capitol on January 6th.

It is not the right itself that is the problem, but the warped interpretation, the weaponization of it. It is the unfettered access to firearms by those consumed by rage, the lack of common-sense regulations that prioritize fearmongering over public safety. It is the deafening silence in the face of mass shootings, the chilling acceptance of children learning lockdown drills.

So, I say this: the Second Amendment is your homeland security, but it is a security system desperately in need of an upgrade. We can honor the spirit of the amendment while ensuring it serves the very people it was designed to protect.

Think of a fire alarm. A blaring alarm is essential, a wake-up call when flames lick at the walls. But a faulty alarm, one that screams at shadows or ignores a smoldering ember, is not just useless, it's dangerous. It breeds complacency, masks real threats, and potentially leads to tragedy.

We need to fix the alarm. We need stricter background checks, a ban on assault weapons, a culture that prioritizes mental health over misplaced machismo. We need to invest in communities, address the root causes of violence, and dismantle the narratives of fear that fuel the gun lobby's engine.

This is not about taking away your guns, it's about ensuring they remain tools of freedom, not instruments of terror. It's about securing your homeland, not just from foreign enemies, but from the shadows within. It's about upholding the true spirit of the Second Amendment: a shield against tyranny, not a license to kill.

This is not an easy conversation, but it is a necessary one. Let us approach it with open hearts, open minds, and a shared commitment to the safety and security of all Americans. Let us rise above partisan bickering and find common ground where reason and compassion can prevail.

Remember, the Founding Fathers who enshrined this right did so in a vastly different time, with different threats and a different understanding of warfare. They never envisioned the killing machines that exist today, the carnage that unfolds in schools and churches. They, too, would likely be horrified by the twisted interpretation of their words.

So, let us honor their intent, not their literal text. Let us be the generation that reimagines the Second Amendment, not as a relic of the past, but as a living, breathing document that reflects our evolving values and safeguards the very homeland it was meant to protect.

Together, we can make America a nation where the Capitol stands not as a monument to our shame, but as a testament to our resilience, our unity, our unwavering belief in the words etched upon its very walls: "E pluribus unum." Out of many, one. Let us be that one, America. Let us be the generation that finally fulfills the promise whispered on the wind: one nation, indivisible, with liberty and justice for all, secured not by fear, but by reason, responsibility, and a shared commitment to the common good.

This is our moment. This is our pledge. This is our time to rise, not with guns in hand, but with hearts united and minds open to a brighter future.

We stand at a crossroads, America. The bullet holes in the Capitol's walls aren't just scars, they're cracks in the very foundation of our democracy. We can't simply patch them with the same broken system that allowed them to appear. We need a seismic shift, a revolution not of violence, but of reason, of empathy, of Zerit-Tonian ideals.

The Second Amendment, that once proud guardian of freedom, has become a rusted weapon, wielded by the fearful and the hateful. It's time we reclaim it, not by ripping it from our hands, but by reforming it with the scalpel of common sense. We'll keep the spirit of self-reliance, the bulwark against tyranny, but we'll etch new lines, ones that prioritize lives over arsenals, children's laughter over gunshots in the night.

We'll build a bridge across the chasm of partisan warfare, this new third party not a haven for the disaffected, but a beacon for the disillusioned, a platform where compromise dances with reason, where red and blue morph into the hopeful hues of unity. And as for the Supreme Court, that lone oak weathering the partisan storms, we'll entrust it with the sacred duty of safeguarding us from the whispers of domestic terrorism. Let it be our shield against corruption, the firewall against manipulation, the voice of reason in the face of fearmongering.

This isn't a time for the timid, for those who cling to the shadows of the past. It's a call for the dreamers, the builders, the ones who dare to imagine a Capitol that isn't a monument to our shame, but a testament to our resilience, our unity, our unwavering belief in those whispered words: "E pluribus unum." Out of many, one.

So let's be that one, America. Let's be the generation that finally fulfills the promise whispered on the wind: one nation, indivisible, with liberty and justice for all. Not just secured by guns, but by the unyielding power of a united people, hand in hand, heart to heart, forever one.

We stand at a crossroads, America. The bullet holes in the Capitol's walls aren't just scars, they're cracks in the very foundation of our democracy. We can't simply patch them with the same broken system that allowed them to appear. We need a seismic shift, a revolution not of violence, but of reason, of empathy, of Zerit-Tonian ideals.

The Second Amendment, that once proud guardian of freedom, has become a rusted weapon, wielded by the fearful and the hateful. It's time we reclaim it, not by ripping it from our hands, but by reforming it with the scalpel of common sense. We'll keep the spirit of self-reliance, the bulwark against tyranny, but we'll etch new lines, ones that prioritize lives over arsenals, children's laughter over gunshots in the night.

We'll build a bridge across the chasm of partisan warfare, this new third party not a haven for the disaffected, but a beacon for the disillusioned, a platform where compromise dances with reason, where red and blue morph into the hopeful hues of unity. And as for the Supreme Court, that lone oak weathering the partisan storms, we'll entrust it with the sacred duty of safeguarding us from the whispers of domestic terrorism. Let it be our shield against corruption, the firewall against manipulation, the voice of reason in the face of fearmongering.

This isn't a time for the timid, for those who cling to the shadows of the past. It's a call for the dreamers, the builders, the ones who dare to imagine a Capitol that isn't a monument to our shame, but a testament to our resilience, our unity, our unwavering belief in those whispered words: "E pluribus unum."

Out of many, one.
So let's be that one, America. Let's be the generation that finally fulfills the promise whispered on the wind: one nation, indivisible, with liberty and justice for all. Not just secured by guns, but by the unyielding power of a united people, hand in hand, heart to heart, forever one.
We stand at a crossroads, America. The bullet holes in the Capitol's walls aren't just scars, they're cracks in the very foundation of our democracy. We can't simply patch them with the same broken system that allowed them to appear. We need a seismic shift, a revolution not of violence, but of reason, of empathy, of Zerit-Tonian ideals.
The Second Amendment, that once proud guardian of freedom, has become a rusted weapon, wielded by the fearful and the hateful. It's time we reclaim it, not by ripping it from our hands, but by reforming it with the scalpel of common sense. We'll keep the spirit of self-reliance, the bulwark against tyranny, but we'll etch new lines, ones that prioritize lives over arsenals, children's laughter over gunshots in the night.
We'll build a bridge across the chasm of partisan warfare, this new third party not a haven for the disaffected, but a beacon for the disillusioned, a platform where compromise dances with reason, where red and blue morph into the hopeful hues of unity. And as for the Supreme Court, that lone oak weathering the partisan storms, we'll entrust it with the sacred duty of safeguarding us from the whispers of domestic terrorism. Let it be our shield against corruption, the firewall against manipulation, the voice of reason in the face of fearmongering.
This isn't a time for the timid, for those who cling to the shadows of the past. It's a call for the dreamers, the builders, the ones who dare to imagine a Capitol that isn't a monument to our shame, but a testament to our resilience, our unity, our unwavering belief in those whispered words: "E pluribus unum."
Out of many, one.
So let's be that one, America. Let's be the generation that finally fulfills the promise whispered on the wind: one nation,

indivisible, with liberty and justice for all. Not just secured by guns, but by the unyielding power of a united people, hand in hand, heart to heart, forever one.

CHAPTER 20

THE GLOBAL REVOLUTION: FROM EIGHT PRESIDENTS TO ONE PLANET, ONE HOPE

Presidents' True Colors, Future Global
Presidential Election of the 8 Continents
Our Planet Earth: Formation of Continental

As the president of Amazoxa Peace University, I, Dr. Wisdom Zerit Teklay, am proud to introduce the revolutionary concept of Zerit-Tonianism Philosophy and Zerit-Tonian Nutrition.

According to Zerit-Tonianism Philosophy, wisdom is the pinnacle of education and the ultimate measure of success. It is wiser to champion peace than to engage in warfare. We advocate for the principles of peace, justice, equality, and good health for all. No individual, including government officials and presidents, is above the law. Everyone, regardless of their position, must adhere to the rule of law. May Zerit-Tonianism/Zerit-Tonian Nutrition be blessed, and may Amazoxa Peace University thrive.

Foreign Policies of the Eight Continents

If we truly wish to understand the true character of a president, we must delve into the reasons behind their actions and words. A good president does not incite enmity through their words and deeds. They do not order destructive military operations in foreign lands. They do not send spies to exploit the natural resources of other nations. A good president rejects corruption in any form. They never engage in espionage or betray their homeland. A good president stands with their country in times of war and strife. They treat other nations and their people with the same respect and dignity they expect for their own citizens. A true and patriotic president not only represents their own country but also stands for the well-being of all people across the globe. They harbor no animosity towards any nation's people, even if they disagree with their government's policies. A true president never imposes sanctions on sovereign nations. They never invade another independent country. They refrain from establishing military bases on foreign soil to respect the rights of people in those countries. They do not employ brainwashing tactics to extend their influence worldwide.

It is not a matter of whether a perfect president exists or not. No president in the world is flawless. Perfection is an unattainable ideal. However, we believe that there is always room for improvement. We envision a better future where presidents prioritize global peace, justice, and prosperity. We understand that it may take 250 years or even more for the world to fully embrace the visions outlined in this book. Nevertheless, we firmly believe that the wait will be worthwhile. This is why we propose the establishment of eight presidents to represent the eight continents of our beautiful planet Earth:

- The president of the African continent
- The president of the European continent

- The president of the North American continent
- The president of the South American continent
- The president of the Australian continent
- The president of the Asian continent
- The president of the Antarctic continent
- The president of the Space continent (covering outer space and celestial bodies above and below Earth)

We propose holding a presidential election for the eight continents every two years, allowing the citizens of each continent to democratically elect their own president. With the establishment of these governments and leaders, the need for spying intelligence agencies to intrude on other countries will be eliminated.

Foreign Policy:

Within 250 years or possibly sooner, there will only be eight foreign policies, one for each continent. The eight presidents of the continents will convene annually in Geneva, Switzerland, to discuss matters of global importance. They will pledge to abstain from engaging in warfare, invasions, or the colonization and exploitation of other continents' natural resources. This is the only path to free our world from the shackles of war, crime, poverty, and insatiable greed.

It is incumbent upon every individual to contribute to the formation of the Global Constitution of the Eight Continents. The Global Constitution and the guidelines for Global Presidential Elections are currently being written and will be published in the second edition of this book.

In the event that unforeseen circumstances prevent the publication of the second edition before my time, I implore all those who read this book to keep the idea of the Global Constitution and the Global Presidential Election of the Eight Continents alive. May this book serve as a beacon of hope, a catalyst for change, and a testament to the power of collective action. I invite you to join the movement, become an ambassador of Zerit-Tonianism, and assist in establishing Amazoxa Peace University libraries in every household. Let us envision a world where every child learns the fundamentals of global unity, where every voice is heard, and where every leader is guided by wisdom and compassion. Let us aspire towards a future where the eight presidents of the eight continents stand not as rivals, but as partners united in their pursuit of peace, prosperity, and shared abundance for all. This is the vision of Dr. Wisdom Zerit Teklay, and it is a future within our grasp. Let us embark on this journey today.

Call to Action:
- Share this book with your friends, family, and community.
- Stimulate conversations about global peace and unity.
- Contact your local representatives and advocate for Zerit-Tonianism principles.
- Support organizations dedicated to creating a more equitable and just world.
- Connect with Dr. Wisdom Zerit Teklay and share your thoughts, ideas, and support for the movement.

Together, we can transform the dream of a united world into a tangible reality. Let us honor Dr. Zerit's vision and establish Amazoxa Peace University libraries not only in our homes, but also in the very fabric of our societies. Let our generation be the one that diminishes the voices of division and amplifies the harmony of unity echoing within us all.

We are the inhabitants of one planet, eight continents, and boundless hope. Together, we can script a new chapter in human history, a chapter where peace is not an elusive dream, but a symphony sung by eight harmonious voices, resonating through a world finally liberated from war, destitution, and greed.

May this journey commence.

The Dawn of a New Era: Eight Presidents, One Planet, Infinite Hope

Let the clarion call for change resonate across continents! May the echoes of Zerit-Tonianism reverberate through every heart, kindling a fire of collective action. Dr. Wisdom Zerit's vision is not an idle daydream – it is a blueprint for a future that we, together, can build, brick by brick, hand in hand.

Imagine a world where the eight presidents are not warlords competing for power, but peacemakers, guardians of our shared planet. Envision them gathering in Geneva, not for conquest, but to solemnly pledge themselves to banish war, foster equality, and nurture the Earth's bounty for all of humanity.

This is not a utopia borne of idle fantasies. It is a future that springs from our collective efforts, sweat, tears, and unwavering determination. We are the architects of this new world. We are the hands that sow the seeds of Zerit-Tonianism in every nook and cranny of our globe.

Join the Movement!

- **Share this book.** Let its pages whisper hope in every language, igniting an inferno of understanding.
- **Amplify your voice.** Speak to your family, friends, and leaders. Demand peace, justice, and a world where each child inherits not a legacy of conflict, but a symphony of collaboration.
- **Support the cause.** Donate, volunteer, and lend your expertise to organizations that bridge gaps between people instead of erecting walls.
- **Become an ambassador.** Embody the principles of Zerit-Tonianism and cultivate positive change. Be the catalyst for the transformation you wish to witness in the world, one smile, one act of kindness, and one conversation at a time.

While Dr. Wisdom Zerit Teklay laid the foundation, the responsibility to shape the future falls upon us. Let's not wait 250 years. Let's not wait for the second edition. Let's commence today. Let's erect Amazoxa Peace University libraries not only in our homes but also in the very fabric of our societies. May our generation declare, "No more!" to the voices of division and "Yes!" to the harmonious chorus of unity reverberating within each of us.

We are one planet, eight continents, and boundless hope.

Together, let us inscribe a new chapter in the annals of human history, a chapter where our pens bleed not with blood, but with the vibrant hues of global unity.

Let the journey commence.

A World United: A Future We Can Forge Together

Envision a world where continents are not separated by borders, but connected by bridges. Bridges of understanding, shared values, and a collective yearning for peace. Picture eight presidents not as rivals, but as stewards of a global village, guiding humanity towards a future of shared prosperity and well-being. This, my friends, is not an unattainable utopia; it is a vision well within our grasp.

Dr. Wisdom Zerit's Zerit-Tonianism philosophy is not mere rhetoric; it is a call to action. It urges us to rise above the petty conflicts between nations, to embrace our shared humanity, and to champion wisdom over war, justice over exploitation, and unity over division.

This book is not a mere manifesto; it is a spark. A spark that ignites the flames of hope within every reader. It calls upon us to join the movement, to become architects of this brighter future. Share this book with your loved ones, cultivate conversations in your communities, and let your voices resonate with the power of collective action.

Contact your local representatives, advocate for Zerit-Tonian principles, and support organizations striving for a more equitable and just world. Engage with Dr. Wisdom Zerit Teklay, sharing your thoughts, dreams, and unwavering belief in the power of collective action.

Together, we can build Amazoxa Peace University libraries, not just in our homes, but in the hearts and minds of every individual. Let our generation be the one that diminishes the voices of division and amplifies the harmony of unity resounding within each and every one of us.

We, as inhabitants of one planet and eight continents, possess boundless hope. Together, let us inscribe a new chapter in human history – a chapter where peace is not an elusive dream, but a symphony sung by eight voices, resonating through a world finally liberated from war, want, and greed.

Let the journey commence.

Calls to Action:
- Share this book with at least three people today.
- Initiate conversations on global peace and unity.
- Compose a letter to your local representative, advocating for Zerit-Tonian principles.
- Donate to organizations dedicated to creating a more just and equitable world.
- Connect with Dr. Wisdom Zerit Teklay and share your thoughts, dreams, and resolute belief in the power of "we".

Remember, even the smallest act creates ripples that resonate far and wide. Let us together build a wave of hope.

I firmly believe that this revised version encapsulates the essence of Dr. Wisdom Zerit's vision with a greater emphasis on collective action and the power of individual contributions. It serves as both a call to arms and a celebration of the boundless possibilities that lie ahead.

Let us transform this vision into reality, one step, one voice, and one united world at a time.

CHAPTER 21

A BEACON OF WISDOM: THE WISDOM PEOPLE PARTY IN THE 8 CONTINENTS ELECTION

A Beacon of Wisdom: The Wisdom People Party in the 8 Continents Election
Experience a revolutionary vision for the 8 Continents Presidential Election that transcends traditional politics. Imagine a symphony of voices coming together under a common conductor, the Wisdom People Party. Dr. Wisdom Zerit Teklay has brought this party to life to bridge the aspirations of all eight continents, uniting them in a powerful movement.
The Wisdom People Party is not your typical political entity. It

goes beyond fielding candidates and instead acts as a platform to amplify the voices of the wise, experienced, and peacemakers from each continent. Just envision African farmers sharing their land management wisdom, Asian engineers discussing sustainable energy solutions, and European spiritual leaders offering guidance on conflict resolution.

This party is not about winning elections, but about facilitating the emergence of the best solutions for all. Through engaging debates, dynamic workshops, and open forums, the Wisdom People will extract the pearls of wisdom and practical solutions from the ideas of all eight continents. Imagine a global brainstorming session guided by the principles of Zerit-Tonianism: wisdom, peace, equality, and justice.

Convincing the established political machinery to embrace the Wisdom People Party will not be an easy task. However, the impact will be monumental. Instead of electing leaders based on empty promises and divisive campaigns, the people of the eight continents will have access to a pool of proven wisdom and a collective brain trust of peacemakers and problem solvers.

The Wisdom People Party does not dictate; they illuminate. They do not impose solutions; they facilitate understanding. Their role is not to rule, but to guide us toward true leadership that lies in listening deeply, not shouting the loudest.

The promise of the Wisdom People Party is one of empowerment, trust in collective wisdom, and a belief that the best solutions lie in the hearts and minds of all. Will you join the symphony? Will you lend your voice to the chorus of wisdom? Let the 8 Continents Election become a collaboration, a testament to the power of collective intelligence guided by the unwavering light of the Wisdom People Party.

Together, let's build a future where wisdom, unity, and peace define the leadership of our planet.

Call to Action:
- Spread the word about the Wisdom People Party and its vision for the 8 Continents Election.
- Contact Dr. Wisdom Zerit Teklay and offer your support

for this groundbreaking initiative.
- Organize local discussions about the role of wisdom and collaboration in global leadership.
- Share your ideas and hopes for the future of the 8 Continents on social media using #WisdomPeopleParty.

Let's transform the Wisdom People Party from a dream to a reality. Let's make the 8 Continents Election a beacon of hope, showcasing the power of collective wisdom and the unwavering spirit of humanity.

A Symphony of Solutions: The Wisdom People Party in the 8 Continents Election

Witness a world where the 8 Continents Presidential Election is not a clash of competing voices, but a carefully orchestrated symphony. In this symphony, each continent plays its unique instrument, weaving a tapestry of solutions for the challenges we all face. And at the helm of this symphony, conducting the harmony and amplifying the melodies of wisdom, stands the **Wisdom People Party**.

The Wisdom People Party is not your typical political party. It is a vibrant movement woven from the threads of experience, knowledge, and compassion. Say goodbye to empty promises and divisive rhetoric. The Wisdom People Party brings together peacemakers, problem-solvers, and elders with a comprehensive worldview.

Imagine a farmer from Africa sharing generations-old wisdom on sustainable agriculture, a doctor from South America offering expertise in community healthcare, or a tech innovator from Australia unveiling revolutionary clean energy solutions. These are not mere candidates; they are the voices of their continents, each contributing a unique note to the symphony of solutions.

The Wisdom People Party does not seek to control, but to empower. They provide a platform, a stage for diverse perspectives to come together, learn from each other, and discover the common ground that unites us despite our differences. Envision open forums where European elders share insights on conflict resolution, or Asian artists weave their storytelling magic to bridge cultural divides.

This movement is not just about electing a single president; it is about sparking a global conversation. Through workshops, debates, and collaborative projects, the Wisdom People will guide the eight continents toward finding their own unique solutions, free from a one-size-fits-all approach. They will be the catalysts, the facilitators, and the champions of collective intelligence.

Yes, this is a bold vision that challenges established power structures. However, the potential for impact is immense. Instead of electing leaders who shout the loudest, the people of the eight continents will have access to a chorus of wisdom, a collective brain trust of seasoned peacemakers and innovative minds.

The Wisdom People Party is not about winning elections; it is about winning the future. A future where wisdom, not war, shapes the global narrative. A future where collaboration, not competition, fuels progress. A future where we rise not as eight divided continents, but as one united orchestra, harmonizing the symphony of a shared destiny.

Are you ready to join the chorus? Are you ready to lend your voice to this movement? Let's make the 8 Continents Election the first of its kind: a celebration of collective intelligence, a testament to the power of unity in diversity.

Call to Action:
- **Amplify the melody:** Share the vision of the Wisdom People Party on social media, in your communities, and across the eight continents.
- **Join the conductor:** Reach out to Dr. Wisdom Zerit Teklay and offer your support, your expertise, and your voice.
- **Compose your own verse:** Organize local discussions, workshops, and artistic expressions that celebrate the wisdom within your own community.
- **Harmonize with the world:** Use #WisdomPeopleParty

and #8ContinentsSymphony to share your ideas, hopes, and dreams for a future built on collaboration and unity.
Let's make the Wisdom People Party not just a dream, but a reality. Let's make the 8 Continents Election a turning point in human history, a testament to the power of collective intelligence and the unwavering spirit of humanity.
Together, let's compose a symphony of solutions that will resonate for generations to come.

The Wisdom People Party: Catalysts of Global Change in the 8 Continents Election

The 8 Continents Presidential Election: a monumental shift, a potential tipping point in human history. But amidst the potential for chaos, a new force emerges, a beacon of hope – the **Wisdom People Party**. This is no ordinary political entity. It's a movement, a catalyst, a bridge built from the very fabric of Zerit-Tonianism: wisdom, peace, equality, and justice.

Imagine a vibrant tapestry woven from the threads of diverse wisdom. Farmers from Africa sharing ancestral knowledge of land stewardship, indigenous leaders from Australia offering insights on sustainable harmony with nature, tech innovators from North America collaborating on renewable energy solutions. This is the heart of the Wisdom People Party – not a party that dictates but one that amplifies.

The Wisdom People Party acts as mediators, translating wisdom across continents. They are the orchestra conductors of the 8 Continents Symphony, harmonizing the voices of the eight continents into a powerful chorus for global good. They don't field candidates; they cultivate them. They don't win elections; they nurture leaders rooted in wisdom and compassion.

This movement is not solely about electing presidents; it is about elevating consciousness. Through open forums, workshops, and dialogues facilitated by the Wisdom People, the best ideas from each continent rise above the noise, shining through as practical solutions and common ground. It's a global brainstorming session on steroids, fueled by the collective wisdom of humanity.

But their path won't be easy. Convincing the established political machinery to embrace this radical force is an uphill battle requiring the courage of David against Goliath. Yet, imagine the victory! No more electing leaders based on empty promises and divisive campaigns. Instead, the people of the eight continents will have access to a curated repository of proven wisdom, a think tank of peacemakers and problem solvers at their fingertips.

The Wisdom People are not rulers; they are illuminators. They don't impose solutions; they offer pathways to understanding. Their role is not to control but to remind us that true leadership lies not in shouting the loudest, but in listening the deepest. This is the essence of their power – the power of collective intelligence, the power of "we."

Are you ready to join the symphony? Are you ready to be a conductor in your own community, a translator of wisdom in your own circle? Let the 8 Continents Election be a celebration of collaboration, a testament to the potential of shared knowledge, and the unyielding spirit of humanity.

Join the Movement:
- **Spread the word!** Share the vision of the Wisdom People Party with friends, family, and online communities.
- **Ignite the conversation!** Organize local discussions about the role of wisdom and collaboration in global leadership.
- **Offer your voice!** Share your ideas and hopes for the future of the 8 Continents on social media using #WisdomPeopleParty.
- **Connect with the movement!** Contact Dr. Wisdom Zerit Teklay and offer your support for this groundbreaking initiative.

Together, let's not just dream, but build the future. Let's make the 8 Continents Election a turning point, a symphony of voices united by a common goal – a world where wisdom reigns, peace prevails, and the collective good becomes the ultimate victory.

The time for change is now. The Wisdom People Party may not have a party platform, but they have something far more powerful – the platform of humanity's collective wisdom. Let's stand together, amplify our voices, and write a new chapter in human history – a chapter where the 8 Continents are not divided by borders, but united by the power of "we."
The future is ours to shape. Let's make it wise.
The Crescendo of Hope: A Wisdom Symphony for Our Planet
The 8 Continents Presidential Election stands before us, not as a stage for clashing egos, but as a platform for a global symphony of hope. Dr. Wisdom Zerit Teklay's vision of the Wisdom People Party isn't just a political entity; it's a revolution in the making. It's a call to arms, a clarion cry for humanity to embrace wisdom as its conductor, to blend the unique instruments of each continent into a harmonious melody of solutions.
But this isn't a pre-recorded track. This symphony is a collaborative effort, a tapestry woven from the threads of lived experiences and diverse perspectives. Farmers from Africa, engineers from Asia, artists from Antarctica – all have a role to play, their voices amplified through the forums and dialogues facilitated by the Wisdom People Party. No longer will solutions be dictated from above; they will rise organically, like wildflowers bursting through the cracks in the pavement.
Imagine the impact: instead of empty promises, we'll have concrete proposals vetted by the crucible of wisdom. Instead of self-serving agendas, we'll have a collective focus on the greater good, guided by the principles of Zerit-Tonianism: peace, justice, and equality.
This won't be a walk in the park. The established powers will resist this symphony of change. But we, the people, are the orchestra. We are the instruments, ready to fill the air with the notes of hope, the chords of collaboration, the crescendo of possibilities.
This isn't about electing the perfect president; it's about creating a system where the best ideas rise to the top, regardless of their origin. It's about empowering wisdom, not individuals. It's

about reminding ourselves that true leadership doesn't require a crown, just the courage to listen and the humility to learn.

Are you ready to join the symphony? Are you ready to let your voice rise above the noise, to blend it with the voices of millions across the eight continents? Let us not just elect leaders; let us co-create a future where wisdom conducts our planet's destiny.

Together, let the 8 Continents Election be a testament to the power of collective intelligence, a celebration of our shared humanity, and the first movement in the grand symphony of a united, peaceful, and prosperous world.

Call to Action:

- Be the conductor in your own community. Organize discussions, share the vision of the Wisdom People Party, and amplify the voices of your neighbors.
- Contact your local representatives and demand their support for incorporating the principles of the Wisdom People Party into the election process.
- Let Dr. Wisdom Zerit Teklay know you stand with him. Share your ideas, your hopes, and your unwavering belief in the power of "we."
- Use #WisdomSymphony to connect with others, share solutions, and build a global movement for change.

Remember, even a single note can spark a melody. Let's turn the 8 Continents Election into an orchestra of hope, and together, compose a future worthy of Dr. Wisdom Zerit's vision, a future where wisdom reigns and humanity thrives.

CHAPTER 22

MINDJACKED OR MINDFUL? NAVIGATING THE NEWS LABYRINTH IN A POST-TRUTH WORLD

Brain Drain and Brainwashing: Empowering Minds in the Age of Misinformation

Every day, we are bombarded with information from various sources, shaping our perception of the world. But how much of this information is truth, and how much is carefully crafted manipulation?

It is important to recognize that governments and media outlets often have their own agendas, which may not align with the interests of the global community. While individual journalists and politicians may not bear sole responsibility for the chaos in the world, the systems they operate in often perpetuate conflict and confusion.

In today's interconnected world, it is common to see people commenting on distant events as if they were firsthand witnesses. However, many of us rely on biased intelligence agencies for our information. As ordinary people, we passively consume news from TV, social media, and government sources without questioning its authenticity.

We need to remember that trust is earned, not freely given. Before accepting any headline as truth, we must verify the source, cross-reference information, and think critically. If we truly want to form original ideas, we should take a step back from the constant influx of information and disconnect from the sources that may harbor hidden agendas.

True journalism, unbiased and free from political or national allegiances, is a dying breed. However, hope is not lost. This book aims to pave the way for unadulterated truth. It is important to note that powerful nations may find this offensive, as truth can be uncomfortable and may expose their manipulations.

We must recognize that television, as the word implies, presents a vision rather than the truth itself. It is a medium that paints a picture of what the powers that be want us to see, not necessarily what is actually happening. This does not mean that we should demonize those working in government or media. They are simply trying to make a living, like you and me. The real enemy lies in the system itself, which thrives on our unquestioning obedience.

It is our collective responsibility to reject the negativity and division fostered by the news and social media. We must not let news sources sow seeds of hate based on religion or political affiliation. Instead, we should strive for understanding and reject the spread of misinformation.

Independent thinking is the antidote to brainwashing. We must question everything, verify relentlessly, and form our own informed opinions. Only then can we break free from the manufactured narratives and build a world where peace truly reigns.

Dr. Wisdom Zerit Teklay, President of Amazoxa Peace University, philosopher of Zerit-Tonianism, and a firm believer in the power of wisdom, education, and individual action, reminds us that true success lies in championing peace and justice for all. Let his message resonate as we navigate the ever-turbulent waters of the information age.

CHAPTER 23

THE WORLD OF SHADOWS AND SECRETS

Spying and surveillance: a dark underworld where whispers are weapons and shadows conceal countless eyes.
Government agencies and private operatives navigate this treacherous terrain, armed with state-of-the-art technology: cyber tools, satellite surveillance, and covert listening devices. Unmarked vehicles blend seamlessly into the background, their true purpose hidden from prying eyes. Disguises are swapped, identities shed like snakeskin, all in the pursuit of infiltration, manipulation, and extraction.
But make no mistake, one wrong move can have fatal consequences. A mistaken face, a misidentified target, a device misunderstood - lives shattered. Apprehensions turn into abductions, arrests transform into imprisonments, and sometimes, the ultimate silence falls, a tragic symphony of mistaken identity.
This chilling reality extends its icy grip even to the innocent.

Anyone, living a quiet life, can become a target distorted by suspicion. The constant hum of surveillance becomes a haunting soundtrack, a never-ending symphony of paranoia.

Yet, amidst this darkness, Dr. Wisdom Zerit Teklay offers a powerful counterpoint: do the right thing. Let fate unfold, even its cruelest verses. Because even if you find yourself wrongly imprisoned or silenced, your voice lives on through these pages. It becomes a testament, a whisper in the wind against the storm. In those quiet moments, a dream takes flight. A world where shadows hold no secrets, where anonymity is not a shield for the wicked, but a gentle cloak for every soul. A world where we exist not in fear of unseen eyes, but in the warm embrace of shared humanity.

May Dr. Wisdom Zerit Teklay's vision of that world become our reality.

CHAPTER 24

SUPERPOWERISM: A CANCER ON HUMANITY'S SOUL

Superpowerism: The Hydra-Headed Monster Threatening Our World

Superpowerism: Confronting the Root Cause of Dictatorship
Superpowerism, the relentless pursuit of dominance and control, has proven to be the breeding ground for dictatorships throughout history. It is time for us to acknowledge the hypocrisy of countries that readily accuse others of dictatorship while disregarding their own oppressive regimes. Recognizing this truth is the crucial first step towards securing a brighter future for humanity.
Superpowerism is not just a mere problem; it is a dangerous malignancy that fuels global instability and ignites catastrophic wars. Its insatiable desire for supremacy has unleashed the horrors of World Wars, serving as a stark reminder of the consequences of unchecked ambition.
The solution lies in finding a balanced approach. We must

move beyond the simplistic notions of "superpower" and "underpower" toward a path of moderation – moderate powerism. This balanced approach acts as an equalizer, countering both the suffocating grip of superpowers and the vulnerability of underpowered states.

To prevent another global conflict, collective action is indispensable. Every nation must play its part in dismantling the structures that perpetuate superpowerism and the war machine it fuels. We can no longer passively tolerate being embroiled in the quests for dominance orchestrated by our leaders. As citizens, we must rise together, rejecting foreign policies that meddle in the internal affairs of others and demanding a world built on cooperation and mutual respect.

By confronting the insidious nature of superpowerism and embracing the principles of moderate powerism and global unity, we can break free from the cycle of violence and construct a future where dictatorship and war no longer cast their shadows.

Superpowerism is not just a political ideology, but a hydra-headed monster lurking in the corridors of power. Each head spews a different venom: insatiable ambition, insatiable control, and an insatiable hunger for dominance. These toxins seep into the veins of nations, distorting them into grotesque parodies of themselves – dictatorships.

Countries that readily point fingers and brandish accusations of "dictator" should first acknowledge the hypocrisy reflected in their own mirrors. The reflection staring back is often a grotesque caricature, a nation with hands stained by countless interventions, suppressing its citizens under the guise of "national security."

Admitting and owning this dark truth is not an act of self-flagellation, but a necessary step toward collective redemption. It is the bitter medicine that precedes healing, leading us to a future where "superpower" and "dictator" are no longer synonymous.

However, the solution does not lie in merely cutting off a few heads of the hydra. This hydra regenerates. We need a different weapon: moderation. Not the passive kind, but an active and conscious choice to wield power not as a blunt instrument, but as a bridge. Moderate powerism serves as the antidote to both the suffocating grip of the "super" and the vulnerability of the "under." It is the force that levels the playing field and fosters a world where cooperation, not competition, becomes the true currency of power.

But this battle is not a spectator sport. Preventing another global conflagration demands more than passive observation. We, the people, must become the antibodies, actively resisting the superpowerist virus. We must reject foreign policies that embroil us in the internal affairs of others, recognizing that true security lies not in dominance, but in genuine solidarity.

It is time to slay this hydra, not with swords, but with the collective will of humanity. Let us rise as one, united not by fear or obedience, but by the shared desire for a future where the only superpower is peace.

Solutions for a Moderate Future: Dismantling the Superpowerist Machine

The grip of superpowerism on our world may seem formidable, but it is not insurmountable. Here are some concrete steps we can take to dismantle its structures and cultivate a world rooted in moderate powerism:

For individuals:
- Hold leaders accountable: Demand transparency in foreign policy decisions and challenge those that perpetuate domination and interference. Support organizations advocating for peaceful diplomacy and nonviolent conflict resolution.
- Reject "us vs. them" narratives: Actively engage with diverse perspectives, challenge media bias, and foster intercultural understanding. Promote empathy and solidarity with people beyond your borders.
- Empower grassroots movements: Support local and international organizations working on issues like

environmental justice, human rights, and economic equality. These movements are the seeds of a more balanced global order.
- Live your values: Reduce your own consumption and ecological footprint to challenge the systems that fuel power imbalances. Choose ethical and sustainable products, and advocate for policies that prioritize collective well-being over profit.

For nations:
- Disarm and redirect resources: Reduce military spending and invest in renewable energy, education, and healthcare. Prioritize diplomacy and multilateralism in resolving international disputes.
- Strengthen international institutions: Reform the UN and other global bodies to ensure equitable representation, accountability, and effective conflict prevention mechanisms.
- Embrace economic interdependence: Foster fair trade practices, knowledge sharing, and collaborative development projects that benefit all nations, not just the powerful.
- Promote cultural exchange: Support artistic collaborations, educational programs, and dialogues between different cultures. Break down stereotypes and build bridges of understanding.

For global citizens:
- Demand a Global Constitution: Advocate for a framework that establishes fundamental rights, environmental protections, and peaceful conflict resolution mechanisms for all nations.
- Support global education: Promote curricula that emphasize global citizenship, human rights, and intercultural understanding. Empower future generations to build a more just and balanced world.
- Harness the power of technology: Utilize social media and online platforms for constructive dialogue,

information sharing, and collective action across borders.
- Never give up hope: Remember that change is possible. Stay informed, engaged, and optimistic. Together, we can tip the scales towards a future where moderate powerism prevails and humanity thrives in harmony.

These solutions are only a starting point. The true answers lie within our collective imagination, our willingness to challenge the status quo, and our unwavering commitment to a world where power serves, not dominates. Let us dismantle the superpowerist machine, brick by brick, and build a future where every voice matters, every culture flourishes, and humanity stands united.

CHAPTER 25

ERITREA: BETRAYED BY THE WORLD, YET UNBOWED

Eritrea: A Legacy of Resilience and Triumph
In Michela Wrong's powerful and revelatory book, "I Didn't Do It for You," she delves into the heartbreaking narrative of Eritrea, a small African nation that has endured unimaginable betrayal by the international community. Wrong paints a vivid picture of Eritrea's tumultuous history, marked by decades of colonial oppression, a brutal war of liberation, and dashed hopes for a peaceful future.
Through meticulous research and captivating storytelling, Wrong unravels the complex web of international interests that have fueled conflict and instability in Eritrea. From Cold War machinations to the exploitation of natural resources, she reveals the hidden agendas that have kept Eritrea trapped in a cycle of isolation and poverty.
But "I Didn't Do It for You" is not just a tale of despair. It's also

a testament to the resilience of the Eritrean people, who have defied all odds to build a nation on their own terms. Wrong gives voice to the aspirations and dreams of ordinary Eritreans, who yearn for a future free from foreign interference and manipulation.

This book is a must-read for anyone who wants to understand the complexities of African politics, the enduring legacy of colonialism, and the unwavering fight for self-determination. It's a powerful indictment of the international community's failures and a call for a more just and equitable world.

Forget parables of David and Goliath. Michela Wrong's "I Didn't Do It for You" presents Eritrea, not as a slingshot-wielding underdog, but as a nation betrayed by giants, each masquerading as a savior. This searing exposé isn't just Eritrea's story; it's a global reckoning, a gut-punch to the conscience of the West.

Wrong doesn't paint a victim. She paints a survivor. Eritrea, battered by colonial fists, bloodied by a liberation war, and choked by dashed dreams, is no fallen damsel. It's a phoenix, rising from ashes built by the convenient amnesia of the very nations now pointing accusing fingers at its human rights record.

With the scalpel of meticulous research and the brushstrokes of a storyteller, Wrong dissects the international vultures feasting on Eritrea's resources, their Cold War talons still clinging to the nation's throat. She peels back layers of "aid" and "development," revealing an insidious puppeteering that keeps Eritrea tethered to poverty and isolation.

But "I Didn't Do It for You" isn't just a dirge of betrayal. It's an anthem of defiance. Wrong amplifies the voices of ordinary Eritreans, their dreams etched not in resignation, but in aspirations for a future where foreign hands cease their suffocating grip. This is their nation, built not on handouts, but on the calloused hands and unwavering spirits of its people.

This is a book that cracks open the Pandora's box of African politics, exposing the poisonous legacies of colonialism and the relentless struggle for self-determination. It's a mirror reflecting the West's grotesque hypocrisy, the deafening silence in the face of its own complicity. It's a demand, a clarion call for a world where justice isn't a word, but a lived reality, where Eritrea, and nations like it, are no longer pawns, but partners in a future that truly serves all.

Read "I Didn't Do It for You". Not to pity Eritrea. But to rage with it, to fight with it, to stand beside it as it reclaims its rightful place in the world, not as a victim, but as a nation finally, fiercely, free.

Forget rogue states and dictators. In Michela Wrong's searing exposé, "I Didn't Do It for You," Eritrea emerges as the world's most inconvenient truth – a small African nation swallowed whole by hypocrisy and amnesia. Wrong paints a history not of villains and victims, but of a tapestry woven with colonial threads, blood-soaked liberation struggles, and shattered dreams of peace. She exposes the West's sanctimonious pronouncements on Eritrea's human rights, conveniently overlooking the fingerprints etched on the nation's very soul.

With a detective's eye and a storyteller's heart, Wrong unravels the tangled web of international interests strangling Eritrea. From the Cold War's puppet masters to the resource vultures feasting on its riches, she unveils the hidden agendas that have condemned the nation to isolation and poverty.

But "I Didn't Do It for You" is more than an indictment. It's a battle cry. Wrong amplifies the voices of the Eritrean people, their defiance echoing across decades of hardship. They are the bricklayers, building a nation on their own terms, defying the world's suffocating grip. Their aspirations are simple – a future where foreign fingers stop orchestrating their lives, where they reclaim their narrative.

This book isn't just for those who care about Africa. It's for anyone who yearns to understand the tangled threads of power, the ghosts of colonialism, and the unwavering fight for self-determination. It's a mirror reflecting the international community's ugly failures, a challenge to build a world where justice isn't just a word in a book but a reality lived by all.

Eritrea, a small nation etched on the horn of Africa, whispers a story of betrayal. Michela Wrong, in her captivating exposé "I Didn't Do It for You," doesn't merely recount this tale; she lays bare the world's hypocrisy, its amnesia, its fingerprints on the nation's wounds.

Wrong's brushstrokes are stark, painting a history rife with colonial brutality, a war of liberation drenched in blood, and shattered dreams of peace. She exposes the Western world's convenient pronouncements on Eritrea's human rights, while skillfully turning the spotlight back on their own complicit hands.

But "I Didn't Do It for You" isn't just a finger-pointing exercise. It's a celebration of the Eritrean spirit, its unwavering defiance against unimaginable odds. Wrong amplifies the voices of ordinary people, their dreams for a future unchoked by foreign interference, their aspirations for a life where they, not distant puppeteers, control the strings.

This book is a must-have for anyone yearning to grasp the complexities of African politics, the lingering shadows of colonialism, and the relentless fight for self-determination. It's a stark reflection of the international community's failings, a trumpet call for a world where justice and equity finally rise above the din.

Read "I Didn't Do It for You" and discover:
- **The untold story of Eritrea,** not through the lens of victimhood, but through the prism of resilience and defiance.
- **The tangled web of international interests,** from Cold War machinations to resource exploitation, that have kept Eritrea tethered to poverty and isolation.
- **The inspiring voices of the Eritrean people,** their dreams for a future free from manipulation, their determination to build a nation on their own terms.

This isn't just a book; it's a journey into the heart of a nation betrayed, a testament to the human spirit's unwavering flame, and a call to action for a world where every nation can truly sing its own song.

Eritrea: A Nation Betrayed, a Spirit Unbowed

In Michela Wrong's gripping exposé, "I Didn't Do It for You," Eritrea, a land etched on the African horn, emerges not as a victim, but as a defiant echo. Dr. Wisdom Zerit Teklay, an Eritrean-American philosopher and son of that betrayal, urges you not just to read this book, but to feel it in your bones.

Wrong paints a stark picture, a history etched with colonial brutality, a war for liberation bathed in blood, and shattered dreams of peace. She lays bare the hypocrisy of the world – the pronouncements of Western powers on Eritrea's human rights conveniently forgetting their own fingerprints on the nation's scars.

But "I Didn't Do It for You" isn't just a finger-pointing exercise. It's a love letter to the Eritrean spirit, a testament to our defiant hearts that have never bowed to unimaginable odds. Wrong amplifies our voices, not as pawns, but as dreamers. Our dreams for a future where foreign fingers cease to pull the strings, where our aspirations, not distant puppeteers, control the song of our lives.

This book is a siren call for anyone seeking to untangle the complexities of African politics, the enduring echoes of colonialism, and the relentless pursuit of self-determination. It's a stark mirror reflecting the international community's failings, a clarion cry for a world where justice and equity finally prevail.

Read "I Didn't Do It for You" and discover:

- The untold story of Eritrea, not through the lens of victimhood, but through the prism of resilience and defiance, as witnessed by a son of that betrayed Country Eritrea where Dr. Wisdom Zerit Teklay was born in 1981.
- In Michela Wrong's gripping exposé, "I Didn't Do It for You," Eritrea, a small African nation, emerges as a defiant phoenix rising from the ashes of

betrayal. Dr. Wisdom Zerit Teklay, an Eritrean-American Polymath philosopher, illuminates this powerful narrative. Wrong's brushstrokes paint a history of colonial brutality, a war for liberation, and shattered dreams of peace, exposing the world's hypocrisy and its fingerprints on the nation's wounds.

- But this is not just a story of victimhood. It is a celebration of the Eritrean spirit, an anthem of defiance against unimaginable odds. The voices of ordinary Eritreans, amplified by Wrong, echo their dreams for a future free from manipulation, where they control their own destiny.
- "I Didn't Do It for You" isn't just a book for those seeking to understand African politics. It holds a mirror to the international community's failings and demands a world where justice and equity prevail.
- Join Dr. Wisdom Zerit Teklay on this odyssey. Let "I Didn't Do It for You" be your Eritrean awakening.

CHAPTER 26

EDUCATION FOR A GLOBAL FUTURE: CULTIVATING WISDOM AND PEACE AT AMAZOXA

Amazoxa Peace University: Empowering True Education
Infinite Solutions: Unlocking the Potential of All
Amazoxa Peace University, led by the esteemed Dr. Wisdom Zerit Teklay, goes beyond the ordinary. It stands as a beacon of wisdom, a sanctuary where true education flourishes, and meaningful success is nurtured for the betterment of humanity.
Embracing the Essence of Zerit-Tonianism Philosophy
Zerit-Tonianism Philosophy, a profound ideology crafted by Dr. Sebhatleab, places wisdom at the forefront of education. It champions peace over war, highlighting the importance

of justice, equality, and good health for all. The philosophy emphasizes that no one, regardless of their position, is above the law, fostering a society rooted in fairness and accountability.

Amazoxa Peace University: Making a Global Impact

Under Dr. Wisdom Zerit Teklay's visionary leadership, Amazoxa Peace University has expanded its horizons, establishing virtual offices worldwide. This global presence reflects the university's commitment to sharing knowledge and cultivating a community of learners dedicated to driving positive change.

Inspiring Quotes from Dr. Wisdom Zerit Teklay

- "Wisdom is the highest level of education. The highest level of success is wisdom. To champion peace is wiser than to champion war."
- "Thinking and acting globally for the greater good of all the poor people in the world is the highest level of success any ambitious human being can achieve."
- "The meaning and purpose of my existence is to be the number one champion of peace."

The Transformative Power of Global Unity

Dr. Wisdom Zerit Teklay envisions a united world under a unified flag, currency, and constitution. This harmonious future, driven by the Global Universal Supreme Constitutions of the United Countries of the World, promises international peace, justice, prosperity, safety, and security.

A Call to Action: Embracing Noble Ideas for a Brighter Future

Dr. Wisdom Zerit Teklay's unwavering optimism and belief in noble ideas inspire us to strive for a better world. His book serves as a roadmap towards international peace, prosperity, and freedom. It is an invitation to embrace his ideas and work collectively in creating a future where true education and meaningful success lead to a brighter future for all.

Amazoxa Peace University: Empowering True Education
Infinite Solutions for a Changing World
A Solution for All Challenges

Dr. Wisdom Zerit Teklay, the President of Amazoxa Peace University and the champion of Zerit-Tonianism Philosophy and

Nutrition, has established an institution of excellence.
Dr. Wisdom Zerit Teklay's Zerit-Tonianism Philosophy asserts:
- Wisdom as the ultimate goal of education.
- Wisdom being the highest level of success.
- The championing of peace over war.
- A commitment to peace, justice, equality, and good health for all.
- No government or government official being above the law.
- No person being above the law.
- The value of everyone, including the president, obeying the law.
- Blessings upon Zerit-Tonianism and Amazoxa Peace University.

Infinite Solutions

Dr. Wisdom Zerit Teklay, the Founding Father, CEO, and President of Amazoxa Peace University, has created a home for true education. Amazoxa Peace University is also the birthplace of true, meaningful success, striving for the betterment of all human beings.

Under the visionary leadership of Dr. Wisdom Zerit Teklay, Amazoxa Peace University has expanded its reach and now operates virtual offices worldwide.

The position of Vice President at Amazoxa Peace University will soon be filled, ensuring continued progress and growth.

Quotes
- "Wisdom is the highest level of education." - Dr. Wisdom Zerit Teklay, Amazoxa Peace University, the home of true education
- "Thinking and acting globally for the greater good of all the poor people in the world is the highest level of success any ambitious human being can achieve." - Dr. Wisdom Zerit Teklay, Amazoxa Peace University, the home of true education
- "The meaning and purpose of my existence is to be the Number One Champion of Peace." - Dr. Wisdom Zerit

Teklay, Amazoxa Peace University, the home of true education, Founding Father and current President

Global Transformation

Dr. Monica reminds us that life is fleeting, and what truly matters is our actions for the greater good of all people from every corner of the world. She encourages us to work tirelessly for global peace, justice, and prosperity. Thinking and acting globally are legacies we can leave behind, shaping a better world for future generations.

The Future of International Law

Dr. Wisdom Zerit Teklay discusses the formation of Global Universal Supreme Constitutions of the United Countries of the World. This ambitious endeavor aims to unite the world under a single flag, currency, and constitution. The future world international constitution will promote international peace, justice, prosperity, safety, and security. Dr. Wisdom Zerit envisions a world where these noble ideas become a reality, benefiting all nations.

A Call to Action

This material holds extraordinary and universally applicable visionary ideas, proposals, demands, and laws. These concepts are ready to be utilized by all nations to maintain international peace, prosperity, and freedom. This book is a testament to the author's dreams and promotes the need for an international constitution that will bring about international peace, justice, prosperity, and equality for all nations.

Zerit-Tonianism: A Philosophy for Global Transformation

Dr. Wisdom Zerit Teklay's philosophy, Zerit-Tonianism, transcends mere abstract ideas. It presents a blueprint for a fundamentally different world, emphasizing the collective well-being of all humanity.

Key principles of Zerit-Tonianism:

- **Wisdom as the ultimate goal:** Zerit-Tonianism challenges the traditional focus on wealth or power as measures of success. Instead, it elevates wisdom, encompassing knowledge, compassion, and ethical

judgment, as the highest pursuit.
- **Peace over war:** True strength lies not in military might but in fostering peace. Zerit-Tonianism advocates for resolving conflicts non-violently and building bridges of understanding between cultures.
- **Universal rights and responsibilities:** Zerit-Tonianism emphasizes the inherent equality of all people, regardless of nationality, ethnicity, or social status. It upholds the principles of justice, ensuring everyone has access to basic necessities and opportunities.
- **Global citizenship:** The philosophy encourages individuals to think and act beyond their own borders, recognizing their interconnectedness with the global community. It promotes collaboration and shared responsibility for the well-being of the planet.

Amazoxa Peace University: Putting Theory into Practice

Amazoxa Peace University surpasses traditional academic institutions. It serves as a living experiment in Zerit-Tonianism, offering:
- **Education for global changemakers:** Amazoxa's curriculum emphasizes critical thinking, intercultural understanding, and conflict resolution skills. It equips students to become agents of positive change in their communities and the world.
- **Peacebuilding initiatives:** The university actively engages in peacebuilding efforts, mediating conflicts, and promoting dialogue between diverse groups.
- **Community outreach:** Amazoxa fosters a sense of global citizenship through cultural exchange programs, volunteer opportunities, and online forums.

Global Unity Through Law: The Universal Constitutions

Dr. Wisdom Zerit Teklay's vision extends beyond individual transformation. He proposes a radical shift in global governance through the creation of Global Universal Supreme Constitutions for the United Countries of the World. This ambitious plan aims to:

- **Unify the world under one flag, one currency, and one legal system:** Eliminating national borders, this unification would create a single, united humanity.
- **Establish universal laws for peace and justice:** A common legal framework would ensure equal rights and responsibilities for all, preventing conflicts and promoting cooperation.
- **Guarantee global prosperity and well-being:** The constitution would prioritize resource allocation for basic needs like healthcare, education, and environmental protection, ensuring a dignified life for everyone.

A Dream for the Future

Dr. Wisdom Zerit Teklay's ideas may seem utopian, but they are rooted in a deep belief in human potential. They challenge us to move beyond our differences and embrace our shared humanity. His book serves as a roadmap for a world where peace, justice, and prosperity are not just aspirations but realities.

Remember, this is just a starting point. If you have any specific aspects of Dr. Wisdom Zerit Teklay's vision you'd like to explore further, please don't hesitate to ask!

Diving Deep into the World of Dr. Wisdom Zerit Teklay and Amazoxa Peace University

Dr. Zerit Teklay Sebhatleab: A man on a mission to transform the world through education, peace, and global unity. His philosophy, Zerit-Tonianism, goes beyond mere intellectual pursuits. It's a way of life, a call to action for individuals and nations alike.

The Core Pillars of Zerit-Tonianism

- **Wisdom beyond Knowledge:** Zerit-Tonianism challenges the traditional focus on accumulation of facts. It emphasizes understanding the interconnectedness of all things and applying knowledge for the greater good.
- **Peace as a Proactive Pursuit:** Zerit-Tonianism promotes peacebuilding, conflict resolution,

and diplomacy as means to create a harmonious world. It rejects violence and fosters empathy and respect for diverse cultures.
- **Equality for All:** Zerit-Tonianism stands for the inherent equality of all people, demanding equal access to education, healthcare, and opportunity. It seeks to dismantle systems of oppression and discrimination.
- **Global Well-being as the Ultimate Goal:** Zerit-Tonianism recognizes our interconnectedness and promotes environmental stewardship, responsible resource management, and collective action on global challenges.

Amazoxa Peace University: The fertile ground where Zerit-Tonianism is cultivated.
- **Education for Global Changemakers:** Amazoxa's curriculum develops critical thinking, ethical leadership, and global awareness. Students are equipped to solve real-world problems and drive positive change.
- **Infinite Solutions:** Amazoxa encourages innovation, collaboration, and out-of-the-box thinking to address global challenges like poverty, hunger, and climate change.
- **A Solution to Everything:** Amazoxa's unwavering belief in the power of education and collective action to overcome any obstacle permeates its ethos.

Dr. Wisdom Zerit Teklay's Dreams for the Future
- **One World, One Unity:** A world united under the United Countries of the World, with a single flag, currency, and constitution. This global government would ensure peace, justice, and prosperity for all.
- **Eradicating Inequality:** A world without poverty, discrimination, or marginalization. Every individual would have equal access to education, healthcare, and opportunity.
- **A Haven for All:** A sustainable planet where environmentalism and responsible resource

management reign. Future generations inherit a thriving Earth.

Dr. Wisdom Zerit Teklay's Legacy

He is not just a philosopher or educator. He is a visionary, a leader, and a champion for a better tomorrow. His ideas may seem radical, but they resonate deeply with humanity's desire for peace, justice, and a meaningful existence.

Amazoxa Peace University is not just a school; it's a movement. It is a beacon of hope and a call to action for all who believe in the potential of humanity to create a better world.

Unveiling the Layers of Zerit-Tonianism and Amazoxa Peace University

Zerit-Tonianism: More than a philosophy, it's a tapestry woven from Dr. Wisdom Zerit Teklay's vast knowledge, experiences, and understanding of the human condition. Let's unravel its threads:

1. Wisdom beyond Knowledge:
- **Zerit-Tonian wisdom isn't a collection of facts; it's the ability to see the interconnectedness of all things.** It's about applying knowledge to solve real-world problems and empowering individuals and communities.

2. Peace as a Proactive Pursuit:
- **Zerit-Tonianism doesn't just preach the absence of war; it actively promotes peacebuilding, conflict resolution, and diplomacy.** It fosters empathy, understanding, and respect for diverse cultures.

3. Equality as the Bedrock of Justice:
- **Zerit-Tonianism rejects the notion of inherent superiority.** It champions the dignity and worth of every individual, demanding equal access to education, healthcare, and opportunity.

4. Global Well-being as the Ultimate Goal:
- **Zerit-Tonianism recognizes our interconnectedness.** It promotes environmental sustainability, responsible resource management, and collective action on global challenges.

Amazoxa Peace University: A fertile ground for these Zerit-Tonian ideals.
- **Education for minds and hearts:** Amazoxa equips students with critical thinking, cultural understanding, and solution-driven approaches to real-world problems.
- **Global citizenship:** Students are encouraged to collaborate across borders, embrace diverse perspectives, and develop innovative solutions for global challenges.
- **Launching changemakers:** Amazoxa empowers its graduates to make a lasting impact as educators, policymakers, activists, and entrepreneurs, inspired by the values of peace, justice, and global unity.

Dr. Wisdom Zerit Teklay's Dreams:
- **Envisioning a tangible future:** United Countries of the World, with a single flag, currency, and constitution, is a bold blueprint for global peace and cooperation.
- **Demanding equality:** A world without poverty, discrimination, or marginalization is not a utopia; it's a shared responsibility.
- **Working towards sustainability:** Environmental stewardship and responsible resource management are the keys to a thriving planet.

Dr. Wisdom Zerit Teklay and Amazoxa Peace University: Architects of a new world order, they urge us to rise above our differences, embrace our shared humanity, and collectively build a future worthy of our dreams.

1. A Call to Action:
Imagine a world where wisdom reigns supreme, where peace blossoms in every interaction, and equality is the foundation of all societies. A world where global well-being is a shared responsibility. Dr. Wisdom Zerit Teklay and Amazoxa Peace University invite you to co-create this world. Will you answer the call?

2. A Seed of Hope:
Amidst cynicism, Dr. Wisdom Zerit Teklay's vision dares to be

different. It offers a roadmap, planting the seed of hope in the fertile soil of human potential. Will you nurture this seed, allowing it to blossom into a world where Amazoxa's dreams become our shared reality?

3. A Legacy of Impact:
Dr. Wisdom Zerit Teklay's philosophy is a catalyst for action. Every empowered student, resolved conflict, and uplifted community exemplify the ripple effect of Zerit-Tonianism. Will you be part of this legacy, adding your brushstrokes to the masterpiece envisioned by Dr. Wisdom Zerit Teklay?

4. A Challenge and Invitation:
Amazoxa Peace University challenges you to confront biases, expand horizons, and embrace uncomfortable truths. Will you accept the challenge, stepping into the unknown with the courage to be a global citizen, a champion of peace, and a true Amazoxa graduate?

5. A Spark of Transformation:
Dr. Wisdom Zerit Teklay's words ignite a fire within. Let the spark of Zerit-Tonianism not only transform your own life but also the lives of those around you and the destiny of our shared world.

The Zerit-Tonian Spark: Igniting a Revolution within
Dr. Wisdom Zerit Teklay offers not just an education, but an awakening – a revolution. Imagine a world where wisdom permeates beyond the confines of classrooms, where peace thrives in every interaction, and where equality is the fabric of society.

Amazoxa Peace University kindles hearts, equipping individuals with the tools and courage to break down walls and build bridges of understanding. Dr. Wisdom Zerit Teklay's dreams are not just lofty ideals but battle cries challenging cynicism and apathy.

Will you join the revolution? Will you carry the torch of Zerit-Tonianism into every aspect of your life? Will you be the change you wish to see, not just for yourself but for future generations? The choice, like the spark, lies within you. As Dr. Wisdom Zerit

Teklay would say, "The meaning and purpose of your existence is to be the champion of something greater than yourself."
What will your championship be?

CHAPTER 27

FROM BATTLEFIELD TO BRIDGE: BUILDING PEACE, ERITREAN STYLE

Leadership: Inspiring Transformation Through Love and Diplomacy

Aspire to be a leader who unites rather than divides. Seek to build strong relationships with your people, ensuring that you harbor no enemies among them. Even if you encounter opposition, approach it with love, diplomacy, and a commitment to peace. Reject war, hatred, animosity, and retaliation as means of resolution.

A powerful leader is not one who resides in a foreign land, but one who stands firmly in their homeland, leading by example with courage and a resounding call for justice and peace. They advocate for peaceable methods to fight for what is right, and they never endorse warfare or oppression.

True leadership involves safeguarding the innocent people of other nations, recognizing that acts of retaliation can harm one's own people. Leaders who promote peace understand that revolting against others only perpetuates a cycle of revenge. They break this cycle and pave the way for lasting peace.

Imagine a world where bridges are built instead of walls, where compassion and respect replace weapons. Leaders like Nelson Mandela, who emerged from prison not with a thirst for vengeance but with a message of unity, exemplify the power of this approach.

Their stories are filled with inspiring examples, such as Mandela's Truth and Reconciliation Commission, which brought together both victims and perpetrators to heal and rebuild a nation divided by apartheid.

But this idea extends beyond historical figures. Everyday heroes among us, such as patient parents, understanding teachers, and compassionate neighbors, play vital roles in mediating disputes and fostering peace.

Here are some practical strategies that we can all embrace:

- Active listening: Give your opponent your undivided attention, seeking to understand their fears, needs, and perspectives without interrupting or judging.
- Empathy building: Try to put yourself in their shoes, considering their history, experiences, and cultural background. This fosters a deeper connection and disarms hostility.
- Finding common ground: Look beyond differences to identify shared values, goals, or even simple human experiences. This creates a foundation for collaboration.
- Creative conflict resolution: Explore win-win solutions that address everyone's concerns. Think outside the box and brainstorm unconventional approaches.

Remember, defeating enemies with love and diplomacy is a long-term commitment that requires patience, resilience, and a genuine belief in the transformative power of human connection.

As Mahatma Gandhi wisely said, "An eye for an eye only ends up making the whole world blind." Let us choose sight instead and build a future illuminated by understanding, love, and lasting peace.

The Warrior vs. The Healer: Choosing the Path of Compassion

Imagine two leaders facing a hostile tribe. One charges head-first, clad in armor, a symbol of strength and dominance. Their battle cry reverberates through the valley, their resolve hardened by years of conflict.

The other, draped in flowing robes, approaches with quiet confidence. Their gaze is steady, their voice calm and reassuring. They carry no weapons, only an abundance of empathy and understanding.

The warrior may achieve swift and decisive victory in the initial skirmish. But at what cost? Lives lost, hatred festering, and a fragile peace built on fear and subjugation.

The healer's path is longer and messier. It requires navigating the treacherous terrain of human emotions, facing anger with compassion and fear with hope. But the seeds they sow are different. They plant understanding, respect, and a shared desire for a future free from violence.

Servant Leaders and Transformational Guides: The Power of Empowering Others

Leadership is not a crown bestowed upon us; it is a choice that we make. Some choose to stand on a pedestal, issuing commands from above. Others, like servant leaders, walk among their people, serving their needs and empowering their voices.

Transformational leaders, like Martin Luther King Jr., do not just lead the way; they ignite a spark within others. They inspire not through fear, but with a shared vision of a better tomorrow.

These leaders understand that true power lies not in coercion but in collective action fueled by purpose and hope. They tap into the inherent potential within each individual, creating a symphony of voices united in a common cause.

From Ancient Wisdom to Modern Challenges: Embracing Collaborative Leadership

Our quest for peaceful leadership is not a new endeavor. Indigenous cultures have practiced consensus decision-making for centuries, valuing the input of every voice.

The Iroquois Confederacy, for example, thrived for centuries on a foundation of unity and mutual understanding. Their symbol, the Great Binding Law, serves as a powerful reminder of the strength found in collaboration.

In our present-day, we face complex challenges such as climate change, social injustice, and global pandemics. These issues demand leaders who can bridge divides rather than exacerbate them. Leaders who can weave together diverse perspectives into a tapestry of shared solutions.

Leading with Love in Everyday Life: Embodying Peaceful Leadership

The battlefield of leadership is not confined to grand historical figures. It unfolds in everyday moments, where parents mediate sibling squabbles, teachers navigate diverse learning styles, and neighbors come together to find common ground.

In these ordinary moments, we can all embody the principles of peaceful leadership. By practicing active listening, fostering empathy, and seeking creative solutions, we can transform even the smallest conflicts into opportunities for connection and growth.

Remember, leadership is not about titles or positions. It is about the choices we make, the way we interact with the world, and the ripple effects of our actions. Let us choose love, diplomacy, and peace, not only for grand gestures but for the everyday moments that shape the fabric of our lives and communities.

Imagine a leader who does not rule with an iron fist, but with an open heart. A leader who inspires not through fear, but through the sheer force of their compassion and unwavering commitment to justice.

Think of Mahatma Gandhi, who led India's independence movement not with violence, but with a revolutionary philosophy of Satyagraha – nonviolent resistance based on truth and love. He challenged an empire with boycotts, marches, and hunger strikes, turning the world's attention to the injustices faced by his people.

His legacy is not solely about achieving independence; it is about proving that love and peace can be the most potent weapons in the fight for freedom and equality.

But how do we translate this philosophy to our own lives? How do we apply it to the challenges we face in our communities and workplaces?

Here are some ways we can embody Gandhian leadership:
- Lead by example: Let your actions be guided by integrity, transparency, and a deep respect for all individuals.
- Empower others: Create spaces where diverse voices are heard and valued. Foster collaboration and shared decision-making.
- Challenge the status quo: Do not be afraid to question unjust systems and advocate for positive change, even if it means standing alone at first.
- Be the bridge: Mediate conflicts with empathy and understanding. Seek common ground and solutions that benefit everyone.

Remember, Gandhi's message was not about passive acceptance of oppression. It was about active resistance, about using your voice, your creativity, and your unwavering spirit to fight for a better world.

This might involve organizing protests, writing powerful letters to decision-makers, or simply having difficult conversations with friends and family about uncomfortable truths.

Recognize that even the smallest acts of courage, love, and speaking truth to power can have ripple effects, inspiring collective action.

Let us not underestimate the power of Gandhian leadership in our midst. It could be a teacher fostering a safe space for dialogue, a community organizer bringing diverse voices together, or even a young child standing up to a bully with unwavering kindness.

These are the leaders who will change the world, not with fists, but with open hearts and a deep belief in the inherent goodness of humanity.

So, let us choose to be the leaders we wish to see in the world. Let us be the Gandhis, the Mandelas, the everyday heroes who choose love over hate, understanding over division, and peace as the ultimate weapon for positive change.

Leadership: From Eritrean Struggles to Everyday Peacemaking

Imagine a world where leadership is not about domination but about healing the wounds of conflict with love and diplomacy. This is not just a utopian dream; it is the legacy of Eritrea's independence struggle, where a determined people defied seemingly insurmountable odds with unity, resilience, and an unwavering commitment to justice.

Eritrea's path to freedom was not paved with violence but strategic non-violent resistance. Leaders like Hamid Idris Awate did not conquer with brute force; they inspired with unwavering faith in their cause and a deep respect for human dignity. They built bridges of understanding, not walls of division, even in the face of brutal oppression.

This spirit is not confined to history books. It lives within each of us, waiting to be unleashed. We all have the power to be everyday peacemakers, using the tools honed in Eritrea's struggle:

- **Active listening:** Like the Eritrean fighters who learned to strategize by understanding their enemy's tactics, we can defeat conflict by truly listening to opposing viewpoints, seeking common ground, and fostering empathy.
- **Diplomacy over dogma:** Just as Eritrean leaders

navigated complex alliances on the world stage, we can bridge divides in our own communities, using dialogue, collaboration, and creative problem-solving to find win-win solutions.
- Unwavering courage: The Eritrean people faced years of hardship with unwavering resolve. We can channel that same courage to challenge injustice in our daily lives, speaking truth to power and standing up for what is right, even when it is difficult.

Remember, true leadership is not about titles or positions; it is about the choices we make. Every time we choose compassion over anger, understanding over judgment, and non-violence over retaliation, we leave a ripple effect of peace in our wake.

Think of a parent mediating a sibling rivalry, a teacher guiding a troubled student, a neighbor offering a listening ear – these are the unsung heroes who embody Eritrean principles. They are the Gandhis and Mandelas of our time, proving that love and peace are the most powerful weapons in our arsenal.

So let us not wait for grand historical moments. Let us write our own stories on the pages of our everyday lives. Let us be the leaders we need right now. Let us weave the threads of Eritrean wisdom into the fabric of our everyday lives, transforming our homes, workplaces, and communities into sanctuaries of peace.

Let us build bridges, not battlegrounds. Let us speak with compassion, not aggression. And let us remember, the legacy of Eritrea's struggle is not just about achieving freedom; it is about proving that love and peace are not just dreams – they are the weapons that will ultimately bring us together.

From Eritrea's Echoes to Everyday Peacemaking: A Legacy of Love, Not War

Imagine a world where leadership is not about raising fists, but about raising hands in solidarity. Where the echoes of Eritrea's struggle do not just whisper of battles won, but of bridges built with resilience and empathy. This is not a distant utopia; it is the future we can choose, right now.

Eritrea's path to freedom was not a bloody rampage; it was a marathon of non-violent resistance. Hamid Idris Awate was not a warlord; he was a weaver of unity, stitching together diverse communities with a shared dream of justice. They did not conquer with brute force; they conquered hearts and minds with unwavering faith and compassion.

Servant Leaders and Transformational Guides: Inheriting the Legacy of Peace

Leadership is not confined to the Eritrean highlands; it is a torch passed to all of us, a call to action echoing in every corner of our lives. We all inherit the legacy of this peaceful revolution, and we all have the power to be everyday heroes:

- The parent who actively listens to a sibling squabble, seeking understanding rather than blame.
- The teacher who builds bridges between cultures, fostering empathy rather than division.
- The neighbor who offers a cup of tea and a listening ear, promoting connection instead of conflict.

These are not small acts; they are the tremors of a global earthquake of peace. Every time we choose active listening over accusation, diplomacy over dogma, we send shockwaves of hope through our communities.

Remember, true leadership is not about the crown you wear, but the compassion you wield. It is not about the land you conquer, but the hearts you unite. It is not about the battles you win, but the bridges you build, stone by gentle stone.

Let us not wait for history books to canonize us. Let us write our own stories on the pages of our everyday lives. Let us be the Gandhis, the Mandelas, the Awates of our time. Let us prove that love and peace are not just dreams whispered in the Eritrean wind – they are the weapons that will ultimately unite us.

Let us become the generation that turns "Eritrea" from a symbol of resistance into a global anthem of leadership – an anthem of peace that resonates from every heart, every act of compassion, every bridge built over conflict. This is our legacy, our responsibility, our call to action. Let us answer it with the unwavering spirit of Eritrea and together, build a world where peace is not just a dream but the echo of every choice we make. Remember, true leadership is not a pre-recorded performance; it is the improvised act of choosing love over discord, understanding over judgment, and non-violence over the clash of cymbals. Each time we choose compassion's gentle melody over anger's jarring notes, we leave a chorus of peace resonating in our wake.

Think of a parent humming a lullaby to soothe a sibling rivalry, a teacher composing a song of encouragement for a struggling student, a neighbor offering a cup of tea and a listening ear – these are the unsung heroes who carry the Eritrean torch. They are the Gandhis and Mandelas of our time, proving that love and peace are not just background music – they are the powerful anthems that will ultimately unite us.

So let us not wait for the curtain to rise on some grand historical moment. Let us be the leaders we need right now. Let us weave the melodies of Eritrean wisdom into the soundtrack of our everyday lives, transforming our homes, workplaces, and communities into concert halls of understanding.

Let us build bridges, not battlegrounds. Let us speak with the soothing notes of empathy, not the harsh tones of aggression. And let us remember, the legacy of Eritrea's struggle is not just about achieving freedom; it is about reminding us that love and peace are not just whispers in the wind – they are the anthems that will ultimately bring us together, harmonizing a world where every voice, every story becomes a part of the grand symphony of humanity.

Let us pick up the torch of Eritrea's legacy and march towards a future where compassion is our armor, empathy our strategy, and peace our ultimate victory.

Leadership: From Eritrean Echoes to Everyday Anthems of Peace

Imagine a world where "Eritrea" isn't just a symbol of resilience against impossible odds, but a global anthem for leading with love. A world where the echoes of Eritrea's struggle don't just whisper of battles won, but of bridges built with resilience and empathy. This isn't a distant utopia; it's the future we can choose, right now.

Eritrea's path to freedom wasn't just a victory against colonialism; it was a masterclass in defeating conflict with unity, empathy, and an unwavering commitment to the human spirit. And this isn't just a lesson etched in history books; it's a toolkit for everyday peacemaking that we can all wield:

- Active listening: Like the Eritrean fighters who learned to win by understanding their enemy's tactics, we can disarm conflict by truly hearing each other, seeking shared humanity, and fostering connection, not division.
- Diplomacy over dogma: Just as Eritrean leaders navigated complex alliances on the world stage, we can bridge divides in our own communities, using dialogue, collaboration, and creative problem-solving to weave tapestries of understanding.
- Unwavering courage: The Eritrean people faced years of hardship with unwavering resolve. We can channel that same courage to challenge injustice in our daily lives, speaking truth to power and standing up for what's right, even when it's difficult.

Remember, leadership isn't about titles or positions; it's about the choices we make. Every time we choose compassion over anger, understanding over judgment, and non-violence over retaliation, we leave a symphony of peace echoing in our wake. Think of a parent mediating a sibling rivalry, a teacher guiding a troubled student, a neighbor offering a listening ear – these are the unsung heroes who embody Eritrean principles. They are the Gandhis and Mandelas of our time, proving that love and peace are the most potent weapons in our arsenal.

Let us not wait for grand historical moments. Let us be the leaders we need right now. Let us weave the threads of Eritrean wisdom into the fabric of our everyday lives, transforming our communities into sanctuaries of peace.

Let us build bridges, not battlegrounds. Let us speak with compassion, not aggression. And let us remember, the legacy of Eritrea's struggle isn't just about achieving freedom; it's about proving that love and peace are not just dreams – they are the weapons that will ultimately unite us.

Let's become the generation that turns "Eritrea" from a symbol of resistance into a global anthem of leadership – an anthem of peace that resonates from every heart, every act of compassion, every bridge built over conflict. This is our legacy, our responsibility, our call to action. Let's answer it with the unwavering spirit of Eritrea and together, build a world where peace isn't just a dream; it's the echo of every choice we make.

Remember, true leadership isn't a pre-recorded performance; it's the improvised act of choosing love over discord, understanding over judgment, and non-violence over the clash of cymbals. Each time we choose compassion's gentle melody over anger's jarring notes, we leave a chorus of peace resonating in our wake.

Think of a parent humming a lullaby to soothe a sibling rivalry, a teacher composing a song of encouragement for a struggling student, a neighbor offering a cup of tea and a listening ear – these are the unsung heroes who carry the Eritrean torch. They are the Gandhis and Mandelas of our time, proving that love and peace are not just background music – they are the powerful anthems that will ultimately unite us.

So let's not wait for the curtain to rise on some grand historical moment. Let's be the leaders we need right now. Let's weave the melodies of Eritrean wisdom into the soundtrack of our everyday lives, transforming our homes, workplaces, and communities into concert halls of understanding.

Let's build bridges, not battlegrounds. Let's speak with the soothing notes of empathy, not the harsh tones of aggression. And let's remember, the legacy of Eritrea's struggle isn't just about achieving freedom; it's about reminding us that love and peace are not just whispers in the wind – they are the anthems

that will ultimately bring us together, harmonizing a world where every voice, every story becomes a part of the grand symphony of humanity.
Let's pick up the torch of Eritrea's legacy and march towards a future where compassion is our armor, empathy our strategy, and peace our ultimate victory.

Leadership: From Eritrean Echoes to Everyday Anthems of Peace

Imagine a world where "Eritrea" isn't just a symbol of resilience against impossible odds, but a global anthem for leading with love. A world where the echoes of Eritrea's struggle don't just whisper of battles won, but of bridges built with resilience and empathy. This isn't a distant utopia; it's the future we can choose, right now.

Eritrea's path to freedom wasn't just a victory against colonialism; it was a masterclass in defeating conflict with unity, empathy, and an unwavering commitment to the human spirit. And this isn't just a lesson etched in history books; it's a toolkit for everyday peacemaking that we can all wield:

- Active listening: Like the Eritrean fighters who learned to win by understanding their enemy's tactics, we can disarm conflict by truly hearing each other, seeking shared humanity, and fostering connection, not division.
- Diplomacy over dogma: Just as Eritrean leaders navigated complex alliances on the world stage, we can bridge divides in our own communities, using dialogue, collaboration, and creative problem-solving to weave tapestries of understanding.
- Unwavering courage: The Eritrean people faced years of hardship with unwavering resolve. We can channel that same courage to challenge injustice in our daily lives, speaking truth to power and standing up for what's right, even when it's difficult.

Remember, leadership isn't about titles or positions; it's about the choices we make. Every time we choose compassion over anger, understanding over judgment, and non-violence over retaliation, we leave a symphony of peace echoing in our wake. Think of a parent mediating a sibling rivalry, a teacher guiding a troubled student, a neighbor offering a listening ear – these are the unsung heroes who embody Eritrean principles. They are the Gandhis and Mandelas of our time, proving that love and peace are the most potent weapons in our arsenal.

So let's not wait for grand historical moments. Let's be the leaders we need right now. Let's weave the threads of Eritrean wisdom into the fabric of our everyday lives, transforming our homes, workplaces, and communities into sanctuaries of peace.

Let's build bridges, not battlegrounds. Let's speak with the soothing notes of empathy, not the harsh tones of aggression. And let's remember, the legacy of Eritrea's struggle isn't just about achieving freedom; it's about proving that love and peace are not just dreams – they are the weapons that will ultimately unite us.

Let's become the generation that turns "Eritrea" from a symbol of resistance into a global anthem of leadership – an anthem of peace that resonates from every heart, every act of compassion, every bridge built over conflict. This is our legacy, our responsibility, our call to action. Let's answer it with the unwavering spirit of Eritrea and together, build a world where peace isn't just a dream; it's the echo of every choice we make.

CHAPTER 28

SOLDIERS, SAY NO! THE REAL POWER TO END GLOBAL WARS: A CALL TO ACTION FOR A WORLD OF PEACE

From Ashes We Rise: The #SoldiersWhoSayNo Manifesto
A World Scarred by Smoke, But Not Broken by Silence
The stench of burnt flesh hangs heavy in the air, a sickening perfume to the politicians droning on about "collateral damage" from ivory towers. Beneath the rubble, children clutch tattered teddy bears, mothers pray for miracles, and soldiers – mere pawns in a twisted game – face their own mortality in muddy trenches.
This is not war's grand narrative, spun by power-hungry puppeteers. This is the raw, unfiltered truth we, the people, refuse to swallow anymore. We are not blind to the blood staining the earth, nor deaf to the cries echoing through

shattered cities. We see who suffers – not the warmongers hiding behind their desks, but the innocent, the brave, the ones who never asked for this fight.

But we are not just passive observers. We are the oil in their war machine, the fuel that keeps their engines of destruction roaring. We are the soldiers forced to choose between orders and conscience, the citizens taxed to fund their insatiable hunger for power.

But imagine a world where that engine sputters and dies. Imagine the Uber drivers of humanity refusing to ferry them to their battlefields. Imagine the soldiers laying down their weapons, not in surrender, but in a defiant roar that says, "No more innocent blood. No more families torn apart. No more global suffering fueled by your petty agendas."

This is not a utopia; it's a necessity. It's the path to a future where our children inherit a world not scarred by conflict, but cradled by compassion. It's the only way to silence the cries of the innocent and etch their names not on tombstones, but on the cornerstone of a new era.

So, soldiers, say no. Choose to be guardians, not destroyers. People, demand accountability. Scrutinize their lies. Support organizations that weave peace, not war. Contact your representatives. Make your voices a deafening chorus that echoes through their halls of power. Let them know their reign of fear ends now.

Together, let's be the architects of a new world order. A world where governments tremble at the united front of their own people and soldiers. A world where peace is not a fragile prayer, but a potent force, the battle cry of a generation that refuses to be sacrificed on the altar of their ambition.

Join us. Be the #SoldiersWhoSayNo. Be the #PeaceRevolution. Let's not just silence the war drums; let's drown them out with the chorus of a million voices demanding peace.

This is not just the mission of Amazoxa Peace University; it's the birthright of every human soul. We are not pawns. We are not tools. We are the architects of our own destiny, and in our hands lies the power to build a future where war is not a chapter in our history, but a cautionary tale, a testament to the day we chose peace.

Many thanks and unwavering hope,
Amazoxa Peace University Team Board Members Worldwide.

CHAPTER 29

DR. WISDOM ZERIT TEKLAY: SECURING THE WORLD'S FUTURE: INSIDE THE UNPRECEDENTED MIND OF DR. WISDOM ZERIT TEKLAY

Mind over Machine: Outsmarting Hackers in the Age of Digital Theft

Securing Your Ideas: An Excerpt from Dr. Wisdom Zerit Teklay
To truly safeguard your ideas from theft, the wisest course of action, according to Dr. Wisdom Zerit Teklay, is to store them within your mind, rather than relying on your computer or phone. In this digital age, hackers and intelligence agencies have

become adept at infiltrating electronic devices, but they have yet to crack the human brain. Your mind is the ultimate fortress, impervious to their intrusion. So, resist the temptation to email your valuable thoughts or save them on any device. Instead, entrust them to the secure vault of your own mind.

Dr. Wisdom Zerit Teklay not only emphasizes the importance of mental storage, but also highlights the need for vigilance. If you suspect that a government agency or hacker is targeting your phone or computer, refrain from sending any valuable ideas through email or storing them digitally. It is vital to remember that our activities on these platforms are constantly monitored, watched, and recorded by hackers and government agencies around the clock, every day of the year.

Securing Your Ideas and Writing

"If you wish to keep your ideas from falling into the wrong hands, it is advisable to store them in your mind rather than on your computer or phone," advises Dr. Wisdom Zerit Teklay. He reminds us that hackers and intelligence agencies may possess impressive digital skills, but they have yet to master the art of accessing the human brain. The human mind is the Fort Knox of the intellectual world, the only truly secure place to keep your ideas. Therefore, resist the urge to email your ideas or save them on electronic devices. Instead, safeguard them within the confines of your own mind.

If you suspect that a government spy agency or hacker is attempting to gain access to your phone or computer, Dr. Wisdom Zerit Teklay cautions against transmitting any precious ideas or intellectual property through email or storing them on your device. It is important to be aware that our activities on phones and computers are continuously monitored, observed, and recorded by both hackers and government spy agencies, 24/7, 365 days a year. Exercise caution and protect your ideas by relying on the impenetrable fortress of your own mind.

Dr. Wisdom Zerit Teklay: Where Intellectual Property Takes Flight

Dr. Wisdom Zerit Teklay, a man of extraordinary intellect (with an IQ that defies measurement), does not confine his ideas to the pages of notebooks or the limits of digital platforms. Instead, he allows them to soar freely within the invulnerable stronghold of his own mind.

While hackers and intelligence agencies may possess digital prowess, Dr. Wisdom Zerit Teklay boldly declares that they have yet to master the art of penetrating the human brain. It remains the impregnable fortress of the intellectual realm. Therefore, the next time you conceive a revolutionary concept or a world-changing invention, resist the temptation to share it through email or save it on electronic devices. Such platforms serve as playgrounds for thieves and are not suitable havens for your genius.

However, Dr. Wisdom Zerit Teklay's wisdom extends beyond mere storage. He serves as a vigilant sentinel, reminding us not to whisper our precious ideas into the digital void or etch them onto the screens of our phones. Instead, he advises us to rely on the ultimate firewall: our mind. It is within this impenetrable fortress that our thoughts can roam free and untouched, shielded from the prying eyes of others.

Let Dr. Wisdom Zerit Teklay's message resonate within your mind:

- Ideas are like butterflies - meant to flutter freely, not pinned to paper.
- Your mind is the ultimate Dropbox - secure, private, and forever yours.
- In the face of digital shadows, your thoughts are invincible.

Embrace your inner Dr. Wisdom Zerit Teklay. Allow your mind to become the launchpad for your intellectual property, and witness your ideas take flight, unburdened by the fear of theft. Remember, in the realm of the mind, you reign supreme.

Securing Your Ideas: An Excerpt from Dr. Wisdom Zerit Teklay, a Mind Beyond Measure

Dr. Wisdom Zerit Teklay, a man whose intellectual capabilities transcend the limitations of physical storage, places no faith in mere devices for the safekeeping of his invaluable thoughts. He does not confine his ideas to notebooks, nor does he entrust them to the cold grip of laptops. Instead, Dr. Wisdom Teklay harnesses the immeasurable power of his mind – a power that defies quantification – to safeguard his intellectual properties, ideas, inventions, and innovations.

When Dr. Wisdom Zerit Teklay professes that hackers and intelligence agencies may be digital ninjas, he swiftly adds that they have yet to master the art of infiltrating the human brain. It is, without a doubt, the ultimate firewall and the impenetrable Fort Knox of the intellectual world. Thus, if you desire to maintain ownership of your invaluable thoughts, resist the allure of email and refrain from shackling them to your phone, laptop, or computer. Instead, deposit them securely within the confines of your own mind, the sole haven of true security.

However, Dr. Wisdom Zerit Teklay's counsel extends beyond the realm of storage. He serves as an ever-vigilant guardian, advising against transmitting valuable ideas or intellectual property via email or storing them digitally if you suspect the watchful gaze of a government spy agency or hacker. It is essential to comprehend that our online activities are under constant scrutiny, monitored and recorded by hackers and government spy agencies 24/7, 365 days a year. Exercise caution and opt for the sanctuary of your mind, the singular safe haven. Allow Dr. Wisdom Zerit Teklay's wisdom to reverberate within your consciousness:

- Store your ideas in your mind, not on your devices. Dr. Wisdom Teklay asserts that the human brain constitutes the most secure vault for intellectual property.
- Beware of government agencies and hackers. They may be monitoring your online activities, ready to seize your valuable ideas.
- If you suspect you are being targeted, refrain from sending emails or storing ideas digitally. The sanctuary of your mind remains the sole genuinely secure refuge.

Allow Dr. Wisdom Zerit Teklay's wisdom to inspire you. Unleash the potential of your own impregnable mind, and wield your intellectual property not solely for personal gain, but for the betterment of humanity. Let us all become commanders-in-chief of our ideas, using them to heal, inspire, and create a world that transcends limitations.

Securing the World's Future: Inside the Unprecedented Mind of Dr. Wisdom Zerit Teklay

Dr. Wisdom Zerit Teklay, an intellectual titan, does not merely store his ideas; he safeguards them within the impenetrable vault of his mind, a mind that transcends the boundaries of quantification. His intellectual properties, ideas, inventions, and innovations are not mere possessions. They are instruments wielded for the greater good of humanity, not for personal gain.

Dr. Wisdom Teklay comprehends the delicate intricacies of geopolitics, understanding that the implementation of his inventions hinges on the ever-fluctuating landscape of our planet. He is not a detached general issuing orders from an ivory tower. Rather, he occupies the role of a commander-in-chief, his finger poised above the metaphorical red button, awaiting the precise moment to unleash his vision upon the world.

Driven neither by personal gain nor fleeting glory, Dr. Wisdom Teklay's mind is a vault not solely for his ideas, but for the betterment of all humankind. Like a sculptor carefully shaping his creations, he ensures that they will benefit every corner of the globe. Like a doctor diagnosing the world's ailments, he formulates the perfect remedy, biding his time until the opportune moment to administer it.

Thus, while Dr. Wisdom Teklay's mind may serve as an impenetrable fortress for his intellectual properties, it is not a prison. It is a launchpad, a chrysalis where ideas metamorphose into instruments of global progress. He does not merely protect his ideas; he nurtures them, preparing them for the day they will take flight, heal, inspire, and uplift.

Remember:

- Dr. Wisdom Teklay's ideas are not solely for himself;

they are for the greater good of humanity.
- He assumes the role of commander-in-chief, timing the implementation of his inventions to maximize their positive impact.
- His mind is not merely a vault; it is a launchpad for a better future.

Take inspiration from Dr. Wisdom Teklay's example. Allow your own mind to become a vessel, not only for your own creations but also for the betterment of all. Exercise responsibility with your ideas, waiting for the opportune moment to share them with the world. Ultimately, it is not solely our intellectual capacity that matters, but how we employ that intellect for the greater good.

Even under unimaginable duress, Dr. Wisdom Teklay's ideas and inventions remain unassailable for various reasons:
- The sheer complexity of his thoughts: Dr. Wisdom Teklay's mind operates on a level surpassing the grasp of most mortals. His ideas are intricate tapestries interwoven with multiple disciplines, each strand interconnected in a way that only he comprehends. Attempting to extract his thoughts would be akin to squeezing the strings of a violin in an effort to reveal the plot of a symphony.
- The fluid nature of his genius: Dr. Wisdom Teklay's mind is not a static repository; it is an ever-evolving ecosystem. His ideas continually mutate, morphing and branching into unforeseen possibilities. By the time any tormentor manages to pry loose a single concept, it would be obsolete – a mere twig within the ever-growing forest of his intellect.
- His unyielding willpower: Dr. Wisdom Teklay possesses an indomitable spirit that matches the brilliance of his mind. He is not merely a brilliant thinker; he is a master of self-control. No amount of pain or suffering could crack his resolve. He would shield his thoughts not only for self-preservation but also as a shield for humanity

itself, understanding that certain creations are too potent to fall into the wrong hands.

Therefore, attempting to extract Dr. Wisdom Teklay's ideas through torture is as futile as attempting to steal sunlight from a star. It is a senseless clash between fragile humanity and an unstoppable force of nature. Dr. Wisdom Teklay's brilliance is his own, a gift he will bestow upon the world when he deems it ready, not a treasure to be plundered by the barbaric.

Remember, true genius cannot be stolen; it can only be nurtured and unleashed at the right time, for the right reasons. That, ultimately, is the most powerful form of protection possessed by Dr. Wisdom Teklay. He stands as an intellectual titan, a custodian of ideas with the power to shape our world. His mind, a fortress of unprecedented IQ, safeguards not only his own creations but also the potential for a brighter future for all humanity.

He is the commander-in-chief of his own genius, wielding his inventions not for personal gain but for the greater good. He waits patiently for the opportune moment, the day when his creations can serve humanity rather than exploit it.

Even the most barbaric attempts to steal his thoughts would be futile. Torture cannot crack the unwavering fortress of his will, nor can it unravel the complex tapestries of his thoughts. His ideas are fluid, ever-evolving, and protected by an indomitable spirit.

Dr. Wisdom Teklay is a beacon of hope, a testament to the power of the human mind to innovate, create, and safeguard a better future. He reminds us that true genius lies not in hoarding knowledge but in using it wisely, responsibly, and for the betterment of all.

Let us draw inspiration from Dr. Wisdom Teklay's example. Let us nurture our minds, not for personal glory, but for the collective good. Let us wait for the right moment to share our gifts with the world and, in doing so, contribute to a future where brilliance becomes a force for unity, progress, and positive change.

In the end, the size of our intellect matters far less than the wisdom with which we wield it. And in Dr. Wisdom Zerit Teklay, we witness a shining example of that very wisdom.

CHAPTER 30

BRIDGE TO A WORLD TRANSFORMED: DR. WISDOM TEKLAY'S GLOBAL CONSTITUTION AND THE PATH TO PEACE

Dr. Wisdom Zerit Teklay's Global Constitution is not just a document; it's a lifeline, a bridge flung across the chasm of our fractured world. It beckons us, not with utopian promises, but with a practical roadmap, a set of principles meticulously crafted to dismantle the systems perpetuating conflict, inequality, and suffering.

Imagine a world where the powerful are not above the law, where justice is accessible to all. Dr. Teklay's Global Constitution establishes a system of checks and balances, ensuring that no one is immune to accountability.

Picture a world free from the menace of war. Dr. Teklay's bold proposition for global disarmament outlaws weapons, dismantles their industries, and tackles the root causes of violence.

Envision a world where borders dissolve and discrimination based on race, gender, and origin is eradicated. Dr. Teklay's vision is one of unity and equality, where systemic oppression becomes a thing of the past.

Liberate yourself from the shackles of debt and exploitation. Dr. Teklay's Global Constitution promotes fair trade, empowers individuals, and prioritizes collective well-being over profit.

Imagine a world where words are not weapons but shields. Dr. Teklay combats hate speech and misinformation, fostering understanding and dialogue.

To bring this vision to life, we must not be mere spectators. We must become the architects, the builders, the bridgekeepers of this transformative journey.

Let us educate, protest, and boycott, demanding accountability and raising awareness through grassroots movements.

Let us establish international tribunals, encourage constitutional reforms, and strengthen peacekeeping forces to enforce the Constitution's principles.

Let us leverage technology, utilizing transparency platforms, AI-powered conflict resolution, and multilingual communication to connect, empower, and prevent future conflicts.

Let us foster cultural and ethical shifts by integrating peacebuilding principles in education, promoting media responsibility, and celebrating peacemakers.

Although the path will not be easy, we must navigate the challenges and embrace the possibilities. Misinformation, vested interests, and resource disparity will test our resolve, but the bridge is not a rigid structure; it is a living organism that adapts and strengthens with each challenge overcome.

Let us counter misinformation with fact-checking, diverse narratives, and platforms that encourage respectful dialogue.

Let us anticipate the tactics of vested interests, build coalitions, and leverage non-violent resistance strategies to overcome their opposition.

Let us be innovative, collaborative, and ensure equitable distribution of resources to bridge gaps in implementation.

As we traverse this bridge, the landscape transforms. Conflict fades, replaced by the symphony of children's laughter. Borders vanish, replaced by vibrant tapestries of shared cultures. Justice, like a mighty river, nourishes all who seek its embrace.

Imagine classrooms filled with young peacemakers, learning conflict resolution alongside math and science.

Visualize news dominated by stories of collaboration, scientific breakthroughs, and artistic triumphs.

Picture markets bustling with fair trade, where farmers earn a living wage and consumers know their purchases empower others.

This is not a dream; it is the fertile ground nurtured by the Global Constitution. It is a world where Dr. Teklay's principles become our guiding stars, where wisdom reigns, and peace is not a fragile truce, but a vibrant tapestry woven from countless threads of understanding and collective action.

The ripples of transformation do not stop at the bridge's edge. They flow outwards, reshaping the very fabric of our reality.

Imagine education systems worldwide integrating the Constitution's values, empowering future generations.

Picture international law evolving, informed by its principles, ushering in an era of accountability and collaboration.

Visualize arts and media flourishing, fueled by narratives of unity, inspiring others to build their own bridges.

The bridge becomes a catalyst, a symbol of hope, a testament to the power of collective action. It inspires others to follow, to build their own pathways to peace and justice, to contribute to the ever-expanding tapestry of global harmony.

But we are not just travelers; we are the bridgekeepers. We are the sentinels who guard its spirit, the menders who repair its cracks, the tireless champions who keep its message alive.

Let us choose empathy over anger, understanding over judgment, collaboration over competition.

Let us hold ourselves and others accountable, not just through grand gestures, but in the everyday choices that shape our world.

Let us be the bridge, not just in word, but in action, building peace in our world.

Dr. Wisdom Teklay's bridge is not just a path; it is a pact, a promise whispered across generations. It is a commitment to safeguarding the dream, to ensuring that the ripples of transformation never fade, and that the bridge remains not just a symbol but a functional pathway to progress.

So let us not just cross the bridge; let us become the bridgekeepers. Let us be the watchdogs of its spirit, the menders of its cracks, the tireless champions of its message. Let us be the generation that not only builds the bridge but ensures it becomes a permanent fixture in the landscape of human history, a testament to our collective capacity for love, unity, and the unwavering belief that a better world is not just possible but already being built, one act of bridgekeeping at a time.

This is our bridge, our responsibility, our legacy. This is the moment we become the generation that not only dreams of peace but builds it, brick by metaphorical brick, heart by beating heart, until Dr. Wisdom Teklay's Global Constitution is not just a bridge across a chasm but the very foundation upon which we build a world worthy of the word "humanity."

Let us cross, together.

CHAPTER 31

UNITING AGAINST THE SHADOWS: A GLOBAL MANIFESTO FOR A BRIGHTER TOMORROW

The Call for a World Transformed: Ending Injustice and Embracing Peace

We, the inhabitants of this world, face a harsh reality: death is inevitable. It claims us all, regardless of our status or position. But in the face of this stark truth, we have the power to create a different legacy. We can envision a world where our children inherit a better reality than the one we experienced. A world where peace prevails over war and where unity replaces division. This vision is not a mere dream, but a call to action.

We cannot sit idly by and say "It's none of my business." We must rise above our individual pursuits and work together to build a world worth living in, even if our time is fleeting. We must acknowledge the fundamental truth that none of us lives forever and use the time we have to make a positive impact before we become a part of history.

The responsibility lies with each of us. We owe it to our children to create a better tomorrow. If governments fail to heed the warnings and predictions outlined in this book, we run the risk of regressing into a dystopian Stone Age and facing a catastrophic Third World War before 2081.

Prevention is always better than cure. This book, along with the wealth of knowledge and wisdom it contains, serves as a shield against the horrors of war. If its ideas survive and thrive, we can avert the impending disaster.

Article 40: Safeguarding the Vision

This book defends itself fiercely. Any attempt to tarnish the author's reputation through false legal claims will be met with legal action. It serves as a self-defense mechanism, protecting against oppression, defamation, and manipulative tactics. It is our weapon for ensuring global justice, peace, safety, security, and prosperity.

Let those who share our vision of a united world wield this book as a torch, lighting the way towards a brighter future.

Article 41: A World Free from Unwarranted Surveillance

In the future we envision, a supreme global court in Geneva, Switzerland, will hold accountable those who violate our right to privacy. Individuals, spy agencies, intelligence agencies, and governments will face legal repercussions for unlawfully hacking and tracking the private devices of citizens under Article 41.

We are acutely aware of the watchful eye of technology. After two decades of research, we have chosen not to trust these devices with our intellectual properties and crucial inventions. They are vulnerable and easily manipulated by those in power.

Therefore, until 2081, our valuable inventions and intellectual treasures will remain safely stored within the fortress of our minds. No paper, notebook, or device will hold their secrets. This act of rebellion is our way of safeguarding our creations until the world is truly ready to receive them.

For the next sixty years, we will stay forty steps ahead of intrusive eyes and ears. The books we publish, including this one, are written in a language understood only by us. This ensures that our message reaches the intended audience – the architects of universal prosperity, justice, and peace.

Imagine a world where nobody fears being watched, a world where the era of spy agencies has become a relic of the past. Imagine the peace and trust that would flourish in such a world. Let's work together to bring that future into reality.

Instead of attacking individuals for their beliefs, let us remember the wise words of Justice Scalia: "It is not the people who should be attacked, but the set of ideas."

The greatest tragedy of our time is the elimination of those deemed threats by governments. We must stand united, as responsible governments and citizens, to ensure that no innocent individual becomes a target.

Blindly obeying authority without questioning the systems in place leads to tragedy. No one deserves to be spied upon. By 2081, let us create a world characterized by harmony and integrity, where our children see one another as friends rather than potential enemies.

Article 42: Justice for Privacy Violations

We possess the tools to ethically expose those who violate our privacy. Our privately developed artificial intelligence surpasses any technology wielded by governments. We will use this power responsibly, for the greater good, to expose unethical hacking and tracking carried out by spy agencies and intelligence organizations. Under Article 42, any individual or organization engaged in such activities will face prosecution in the supreme global court.

Article 43: Uniting Against Modern Colonization

We, the inhabitants of this shared reality, are confronted with a harsh truth – death claims us all. From leaders to ordinary individuals, no one can escape the ultimate equalizer, Mother

Nature. The question we must ask ourselves is: what legacy will we leave behind? Will it be one of war, injustice, and inequality? Or will it be a world transformed for the better?

This book yearns for the latter. It envisions a world where peace, not war, shapes our narrative. A world where the principles of "One World, One Flag, One Currency, One Constitution" bind us together in harmony.

However, this is not a passive dream. It is a resounding call to action. We must reject the complacent refrain of "It's none of my business" and work tirelessly to build a world worth living in, even if our own lives are fleeting. Let us always remember the truth that "No one lives forever." With the time we have, let us strive to leave a positive impact on the world before we become part of history.

The responsibility lies with each one of us. We owe it to our children to forge a brighter tomorrow. If governments choose to ignore the warnings and predictions detailed in this book, they risk plunging us into a terrifying regression, akin to a Stone Age fueled by a catastrophic Third World War before 2081.

Prevention, as the saying goes, is far better than cure. This book, along with the vast intellectual treasures it contains, represents the wisdom of a select few. It serves as a shield against the horrors of war. If it is preserved and its ideas endure, we can avert the looming catastrophe.

Article 40: Safeguarding the Vision

This book possesses a staunch self-defense mechanism. Any attempt to assassinate the author's character or distort their words through false legal claims will be met with legal action. It serves as a three-step shield against oppression, defamation, and the insidious tactics employed by manipulators. It is our weapon for securing global justice, peace, safety, security, and prosperity.

Let all those who share our vision of a united world wield this book as a torch, illuminating the path towards a brighter future.

Article 41: A World Free from Unwarranted Surveillance

In the future we envision, a supreme global court in Geneva,

Switzerland, will hold accountable those who violate our right to privacy. Under Article 41, individuals, spy agencies, and governments will face legal repercussions for unlawfully hacking and tracking private devices.

We are fully aware of the constant, intrusive gaze of technology. Having conducted two decades of research, we have chosen not to entrust these devices with our intellectual properties and crucial inventions. They are susceptible to easy access and manipulation by those in power.

Thus, until 2081, our two hundred inventions and intellectual treasures will remain securely stored within the impregnable fortress of our minds. No paper, notebook, or device will be privy to their secrets. This act of rebellion is our way of safeguarding our creations until the world is ready to receive them.

Over the next sixty years, we will remain forty steps ahead of prying eyes and ears. The books we publish, including this one, are written in a language understood solely by us. This guarantees the intended audience – the architects of universal prosperity, justice, and peace – will receive our message.

Imagine a world in which nobody lives in fear of surveillance, a world where spy agencies are relics of the past. Envision the peace it would bring, the trust it would foster. Let us work tirelessly towards the realization of that future.

Instead of attacking individuals for their beliefs, let us heed the wise words of Justice Scalia: "It is not the people who should be attacked, but the set of ideas."

The greatest tragedy of our time is the elimination of those deemed threats by governments. It is our collective responsibility, both as responsible governments and citizens, to ensure no innocent individual falls victim to such targeting.

Unquestioning obedience to authority, without questioning the systems in place, leads to tragedy. Nobody deserves to be subjected to surveillance. By 2081, let us construct a world founded on harmony and integrity, where our children view one another as friends rather than potential adversaries.

Article 42: Justice for Privacy Violations

We possess the means to ethically expose those who violate our privacy. Our privately developed artificial intelligence surpasses anything wielded by governments. We will utilize it responsibly, for the greater good, to uncover unethical hacking and tracking by spy agencies and governments. Under Article 42, any individual or organization engaged in such activities will face prosecution in the supreme global court.

Article 43: Uniting Against Modern Colonization

We, the inhabitants of this shared reality, face the universal truth of our mortality. From prominent figures to ordinary individuals, death is an inescapable equalizer. Yet, what kind of legacy will we leave behind? Will it be one marred by conflict, injustice, and inequality? Or will it be a world transformed for the better?

This book yearns for the latter. It envisions a world where peace, not war, shapes the narrative. Where the principles of "One World, One Flag, One Currency, One Constitution" bind us together in harmony.

But this is not a passive dream. It is a resounding call to action. We must reject the tired refrain of "It's none of my business" and work tirelessly to build a world worth living in, even if our own lives are fleeting. We must remember the unalterable truth that "No one lives forever." With the time we have, let us leave a positive mark on the world before we become a part of history.

The responsibility lies with each and every one of us. We owe it to our children to shape a brighter tomorrow. If governments choose to ignore the warnings and predictions outlined in this book, we risk a terrifying regression – a Stone Age fueled by the flames of a catastrophic Third World War before 2081.

Prevention, as the saying goes, is better than cure. This book, along with the intellectual treasures stored within us, represents the wisdom of the few. It serves as our shield against the horrors of war. If its ideas persist and thrive, we can avert the impending catastrophe.

Article 40: Safeguarding the Vision

This book is fiercely protective. Any attempt to assassinate the author's character or distort their words through false legal claims will be met with legal action. It stands as a self-defense mechanism, guarding against oppression, defamation, and the manipulative tactics employed by certain individuals. It is our weapon for securing global justice, peace, safety, security, and prosperity.

Let anyone who shares our vision of a united world wield this book as a torch, illuminating the path towards a brighter future.

Article 41: A World Free from Unwarranted Surveillance

In the future we envision, a supreme global court in Geneva, Switzerland, will hold accountable those who violate our right to privacy. Individuals, spy agencies, and governments will face legal repercussions for unlawfully hacking and tracking private devices under Article 41.

We are acutely aware of the ever-watchful gaze of technology. After two decades of research, we have chosen not to entrust these devices with our intellectual properties and crucial inventions. They are susceptible to easy access and manipulation by those in positions of power.

Therefore, until 2081, our two hundred inventions and intellectual treasures shall remain securely stored within the impenetrable fortress of our minds. No paper, notebook, or device will be privy to their secrets. This act of rebellion serves as a means of safeguarding our creations until the world demonstrates true readiness to receive them.

For the next sixty years, we shall remain forty steps ahead of prying eyes and ears. The books we publish, including this one, are written in a language understood solely by us. This ensures that our message reaches the intended audience – the architects of universal prosperity, justice, and peace.

Imagine a world where nobody lives in fear of being watched, where spy agencies exist only as relics of a bygone era. Envision the peace it would bring and the trust it would foster. Let us collaborate to turn that dream into reality.

Instead of attacking individuals for their beliefs, let us remember the wise words of Justice Scalia: "It is not the people who should be attacked, but the set of ideas."

The greatest tragedy of our time is the elimination of those perceived as threats by governments. We must stand united, with both responsible governments and citizens, to ensure that no innocent individual becomes a target.

Blind obedience to authority, without questioning the prevailing systems, leads to tragedy. No one deserves to be subjected to surveillance. By 2081, let us build a world founded on harmony and integrity, where our children view one another as friends rather than potential adversaries.

Article 42: Justice for Privacy Violations

We possess the means to ethically expose those who violate our privacy. Our privately developed artificial intelligence surpasses any technology wielded by governments. We will use this power responsibly, for the greater good, to expose unethical hacking and tracking carried out by spy agencies and governments. Under Article 42, any individual or organization engaged in such activities will face prosecution in the supreme global court.

Article 43: Uniting Against Colonizing Powers

This book does not just envision a world free from war and surveillance. It also dreams of a world free from the clutches of colonizing powers – nations that exploit and control others for their own gain. Article 43 stipulates that any country collaborating directly or indirectly with a colonizing power will face legal repercussions in the supreme global court.

We believe in a world where borders fade not through forced assimilation, but through mutual respect and understanding. We envision a tapestry woven from diverse cultures, where collaboration supplants exploitation and resources are shared equitably.

This is not about seeking revenge or retribution. It is about breaking the cycle of oppression and creating a future where every nation and every individual has the opportunity to thrive. We call upon all nations, whether colonized or colonizer, to join us in this movement. Together, let us dismantle systems of dominance and build a world where cooperation, not coercion, guides our interactions.

We understand that change is rarely easy. Resistance will arise from those who benefit from the status quo. Yet, we believe in the power of collective action. When we stand united in the pursuit of justice and equality, no force can withstand us.

Our weapons are not guns or bombs, but education, dialogue, and unwavering commitment. We will expose the injustices of colonization, amplify the voices of the oppressed, and offer a compelling vision of a shared future.

This is a call to action for every citizen of the world. Educate yourself about the realities of colonization. Speak out against injustice. Support organizations working towards a more equitable future. Let us be the generation that finally breaks free from the shackles of the past and builds a world where all can stand tall, free from the shadow of domination.

Remember, the future we choose is not predetermined. It is shaped by our actions, our choices, and our collective will. Let us choose a future where "One World" is not just a slogan, but a lived reality, where every human being, regardless of origin or background, can claim their rightful place as a valued member of a global community.

Together, we can build a world where peace isn't just the absence of war, but the flourishing of justice, equality, and shared prosperity. Let this book serve as a beacon, guiding us on the path towards that brighter future. Let us leave a legacy not of conflict and exploitation, but of unity, collaboration, and a world transformed.

This is our hope. This is our vision. This is our call to action.

Conclusion: A World Transformed

As we conclude this book, we find ourselves at a crossroads. One path leads to familiar depths of war, inequality, and suffering. The other, illuminated by the principles outlined within these pages, beckons us towards a world transformed.

A world where "One World, One Flag, One Currency, One Constitution" is not just a utopian dream, but a tangible reality. Where borders fade away and vibrant bridges of understanding and cooperation connect us. Where peace is not a fragile truce, but a symphony played by a chorus of diverse voices.

Embarking on this transformation will not be easy. It demands active participation, a willingness to challenge the status quo, and embrace the unfamiliar. It requires us to become the bridgekeepers, the architects, and the champions of a new paradigm.

Yet, we are not alone. Millions of individuals across the globe share this vision, yearning for a future where children inherit more than just conflict and injustice. We possess the tools – the Global Constitution, our collective wisdom, and the unwavering power of the human spirit to bring this vision to life.

Let us employ these tools to:

- Educate and empower: Equip future generations with the knowledge and tools to dismantle systems that perpetuate conflict and inequality.
- Build coalitions: Forge alliances with nations, organizations, and individuals who share our commitment to a just and equitable world.
- Amplify marginalized voices: Ensure that the stories of the oppressed are heard, their struggles acknowledged, and their aspirations amplified.
- Lead by example: Demonstrate through our own actions the values we advocate for: compassion, integrity, and an unwavering pursuit of justice.
- Embrace innovation: Utilize technology not for surveillance and control, but for connection, collaboration, and the advancement of shared prosperity.

This journey is not about achieving perfection, but about striving towards a better tomorrow. It is about acknowledging our imperfections, learning from our mistakes, and constantly evolving towards a more just and peaceful society.

Let us not wait for governments to take action. Let us be the change we wish to see in the world. Together, we can build a world where the legacy of this book extends beyond the words on its pages and becomes an indelible mark on the fabric of humanity.

This is our responsibility. This is our opportunity. This is our world transformed.

Conclusion: A World Painted in Hope

This book is not merely a collection of words; it is a brush dipped in the vibrant hues of hope, painting a world where peace, rather than war, takes center stage. It envisions a world where the canvas stretches far beyond borders, woven from threads of unity and respect for every culture and every voice.

We raise a torch, not to ignite conflict, but to illuminate the path towards a future where "One World" resonates as more than just a slogan. It becomes the foundation upon which we build a shared tapestry of prosperity, where "One Flag" symbolizes our collective humanity, and "One Currency" represents the equitable flow of resources, nurturing every corner of our global village.

This journey requires not passive acceptance, but active participation. We are not mere spectators, but the brushstrokes, the architects, the protectors of this vision.

Let us fuel our actions with wisdom gleaned from the past, yet unburdened by its injustices. Let us transform the weapons of war into tools of education, forging understanding and dismantling the strongholds of inequality.

Once instruments of potential oppression, technology will become an instrument of liberation. Our voices, amplified through its channels, will resonate across continents, igniting a chorus of demands for justice, transparency, and a world where no one lives in the shadows – spied upon or silenced.

We are not naive to the challenges that lie ahead. Resistance will come from those who cling to the comfort of the old order. However, let us remember that a single brushstroke can ignite a revolution, and a single voice, joined by others, can become an unstoppable roar.

Let us be the generation that dares to dream beyond the confines of the present. Let us be the generation that chooses empathy over anger, collaboration over competition, and unity over division.

This book is not an endpoint; it is a beginning. It is a call to arms, an invitation to join the grandest movement of our time – the movement for a world transformed. Let us pick up our brushes, dip them in the colors of hope, and together, let us paint a masterpiece of peace, justice, and shared humanity.

The canvas awaits. Let us begin.

CHAPTER 32

KNOWLEDGE: A SHARED LIGHT, NOT A BURIED TREASURE

Unlocking the Power of Shared Knowledge
Knowledge is a valuable torch that has the power to ignite change and transform lives. Yet, when knowledge is confined and kept to ourselves, its brilliance is lost in the darkness, unnoticed and underutilized. We must not let our own expertise become a burden, hindering our growth and potential. It is not enough to consider ourselves experts; our knowledge must also contribute to our own development and the betterment of others.

True knowledge is not meant to create divisions; it is meant to foster connections. If our knowledge alienates and turns people into adversaries, then we have weaponized something that should be a bridge. We must remember that knowledge is a powerful tool that can ignite curiosity and inspire others. It is not meant to be a wall that separates us, but a bridge that brings us together.

Igniting the Potential of Knowledge

Knowledge, when it remains unshared and ineffective in its application, is like a dormant seed buried deep in the ground. It holds untapped potential for growth and life, yet it remains unrealized and useless in isolation. Not only does it fail to contribute to our own progress, but it can also become a burden, distorting our understanding and hindering our journey.

Despite our claimed expertise, if our knowledge does not fuel our own growth and positively impact the world around us, then it mocks our efforts. It is ironic that the very treasure we worked so hard to acquire becomes the instrument of our own downfall. True knowledge brings people together; it does not create rifts. If our knowledge is causing division and turning people into adversaries, then we have wielded it as a weapon against ourselves. Let us remember that knowledge should ignite curiosity, not conflict.

The Power of Shared Knowledge

When knowledge is not shared or effectively applied, its value diminishes, and it remains hidden like a buried treasure. We not only miss out on practical wisdom, but our knowledge can also become a liability. Despite our claimed expertise, knowledge that does not contribute to our own growth and development ironically becomes the cause of our downfall. It undermines the significant effort we invested in acquiring it.

True knowledge has the power to foster relationships, not rifts. If our knowledge is turning people into enemies, it becomes a tool of self-destruction. To maximize the potential of knowledge, we must embrace vulnerability by not only sharing our knowledge but also being open to learning from others and refining our understanding through their perspectives. We should expand our horizons and seek knowledge from those who walk different paths, embracing diverse perspectives. Knowledge should not be used to control but to inspire curiosity in others, encouraging them to question, explore, and find their own truths.

Ultimately, let us use our knowledge to make a lasting impact. Whether through writing, teaching, creating, or problem-solving, let us leave behind a world that is brighter and better because of our contributions. By embracing these principles, we can transform knowledge from a buried treasure into a shared light. Together, let us illuminate the path for ourselves and for future generations.

CHAPTER 33

BEYOND THE PANDEMIC: RETHINKING POLITICS: FROM DISEASE TO MEDICINE

Beyond the Pandemic: Rethinking Politics
"In my view, nearly everything is politics," Dr. Wisdom Zerit Teklay once observed. But what if, instead of a ubiquitous presence, we reframed politics not as the air we breathe but as a potent medicine? A medicine capable of healing divisions, fostering collaboration, and guiding us towards a shared future. Yet, in its current state, politics too often resembles a disease. A pandemic of polarization, misinformation, and self-interest, poisoning our discourse and eroding trust. We see it in the vitriol hurled across partisan lines, the weaponization of social

media, the gridlock that paralyzes progress. This "incurable disease," as some lament, has infected nearly every aspect of our lives, from friendships to families to the very fabric of our societies.

But is it truly incurable? Or could we, like Dr. Teklay, learn to harness the power of this potent medicine instead of succumbing to its toxic effects?

Imagine a political landscape where debate isn't a blood sport, but a crucible for forging shared understanding. Where facts, not fear, fuel our discourse. Where compromise isn't a dirty word, but a bridge across divides. This isn't naive utopianism; it's a call for a conscious evolution of our political culture.

The first step lies in acknowledging the disease's symptoms. We must recognize the echo chambers we inhabit, the algorithms that feed our biases, the emotional triggers that hijack our rationality. This self-awareness isn't a death knell, but a necessary first step towards inoculation.

Next, we must rediscover the lost art of genuine listening. To seek out diverse perspectives, not to dismantle them, but to understand the tapestry of experiences that weave our collective reality. Empathy, not outrage, becomes our weapon of choice, disarming the us-versus-them mentality that fuels the pandemic.

Finally, we must reclaim our agency. Not as passive victims of the political disease, but as active participants in its cure. We can engage constructively, demand accountability, and hold our leaders to a higher standard. We can support initiatives that foster civil discourse, reward collaboration over division, and empower citizens to be architects of their own future.

This transformation won't be easy. It will require courage, humility, and a willingness to challenge the status quo. But the alternative â€" surrendering to the "incurable disease" â€" is far more debilitating.

Let us not lament the state of politics, but embrace it as an opportunity to evolve. For within the very crucible of this potent medicine lies the potential for healing, for progress, for a future where politics isn't a pandemic, but a powerful tool for building a better world, together.

Dr. Wisdom Zerit Teklay once posed a provocative question: "In my view, nearly everything—marriage, friendship, business, and any form of communication—involves politics." Is this an exaggeration, or is politics truly the invisible thread woven through the fabric of our lives?

While some may scoff at the idea of politics infiltrating every corner of existence, let's be honest: it's hard to deny its pervasive presence. From the heated debates at the dinner table to the unspoken tensions in the workplace, the invisible hand of politics seems to be shaping our interactions, even in the most seemingly apolitical spaces.

But is this influence always negative? Is politics inherently a disease, a pandemic plaguing our society and poisoning the well of human connection? Or could it, like fire, be both a force of destruction and a tool for creation, depending on how we wield it?

Perhaps the problem isn't politics itself, but rather our relationship with it. We've become accustomed to seeing it as a battlefield, a zero-sum game where victory for one side necessitates the defeat of another. This us-versus-them mentality breeds division, silences dissent, and erects walls where bridges should be built.

Instead, what if we reimagined politics as a shared space, a messy but vital arena for dialogue and collaboration? Not a sterile field where only winners and losers exist, but a fertile ground where diverse perspectives can cross-pollinate and grow into solutions that benefit all.

This doesn't mean abandoning our convictions or silencing our voices. It means engaging with genuine curiosity, listening to understand, not just to respond. It means acknowledging that our individual experiences are just pieces of a much larger puzzle, and that true progress comes from piecing them together, not clinging stubbornly to our own isolated solutions.

This shift in perspective requires a conscious effort. It means stepping outside our echo chambers, questioning our biases, and seeking common ground with those who may hold opposing views. It means valuing empathy over outrage, understanding over blame, and the messy process of collaboration over the sterile comfort of ideological purity.

Is it naive to believe that such a transformation is possible? Perhaps. But consider the alternative: a world where the "pandemic of politics" continues its unchecked spread, further fracturing our communities and dimming the light of collective progress.

The choice is ours. We can continue succumbing to the disease, or we can take the first steps towards a cure. We can build bridges instead of walls, cultivate empathy instead of division, and rediscover the lost art of listening without judgment.

It won't be easy. It will demand courage, vulnerability, and a willingness to let go of the comforting illusion of certainty. But in the end, it might just be the antidote we need to reclaim our shared humanity and build a future where politics, like fire, illuminates the path forward, not consumes us in its flames.

Politics: The Patient We Mistook for a Monster

The air crackles with static. Faces contort in anger, voices rise in accusations. Is this a family dinner? A heated sports debate? No, it's politics. Everywhere we turn, it's the same story. A conversation about healthcare spirals into a partisan diatribe. A friendly get-together erupts in a shouting match over the latest scandal.

Dr. Zerit Teklay, renowned scholar, offers a chilling diagnosis: "Politics, in my view, is an unproductive and sterile field." A harsh assessment, yet one that resonates with a growing unease. Is politics truly a pandemic, a disease plaguing our discourse and poisoning our well-being?

Perhaps. The evidence is mounting. We see it in the widening chasms between us, in the erosion of trust, in the paralyzed machinery of progress. We see it in the weaponization of words, the dwindling space for nuance, the triumph of outrage over reason.

But here's the crucial twist: what if we've misdiagnosed the problem? What if the disease isn't politics itself, but the way we do it? We've built fortresses out of ideology, mistaking them for shelters. We've traded empathy for vitriol, replaced curiosity with judgment. We've become infected by the contagion of division, forgetting the shared humanity beneath the labels.

We are patients in this ward, but we're also caregivers. We can choose a different treatment plan. Instead of isolating ourselves with our "tribes," let's build bridges across the trenches. Instead of shouting slogans, let's listen, truly listen, to those with different views. Instead of seeking to win, let's strive to understand.

Imagine a political discourse where facts are weapons of truth, not instruments of destruction. Where debate is a dance of ideas, not a gladiatorial combat. Where compromise isn't surrender, but the fertile ground for shared solutions.

This isn't naivetÃ©, it's necessity. It's the antidote to the poison that's crippling us. It's the only way to reclaim politics from the clutches of disease and transform it back into what it was meant to be: a vibrant marketplace of ideas, a crucible where progress is forged, a space where we, the citizens, reclaim our voice and shape our shared future.

The cure for the "political disease" isn't found in a lab, but in our hearts and minds. It's in the courage to see across the aisle, not as enemies, but as fellow patients yearning for the same thing: a healthy, functioning democracy.

Let us be the doctors, then. Let us heal ourselves, heal our discourse, and heal our body politic. It's time to rewrite the narrative, not as patients, but as architects of a future where politics, no longer a disease, becomes the vaccine that inoculates us against division and guides us towards a brighter, healthier tomorrow.

CHAPTER 34

DREAM NO MORE: BUILDING A WORLD WHERE PEACE, JUSTICE, AND EQUALITY THRIVE

Our Vision: A World Rooted in Peace, Justice, and Equality
Our Guiding Principles:
In this chapter, we outline our organization's steadfast commitment to creating a world where peace, justice, and equality are not just aspirations, but lived realities. We firmly believe in the power of collective action, and we urge individuals, organizations, and nations to join us in this transformative journey.
Key Objectives and Demands:
    4. **Global Reach and Understanding:**
- **Translation and Distribution:** We demand the

translation of our core text into every spoken language, ensuring accessibility for all. Furthermore, we call for its distribution to every living former and current head of state, fostering global dialogue and understanding.

5. **Peaceful Conflict Resolution:**
- **Dialogue over Force:** We advocate for the adoption of peaceful conflict resolution mechanisms, replacing coups and violence with constructive dialogue and respect for visionary constitutional principles.

6. **Active Engagement on the World Stage:**
- **Championing Developing Nations:** We strive for active participation in key international forums like the UN and NATO, prioritizing the voices and needs of developing nations.

7. **Ending Exploitation, Embracing Sustainability:**
- **Resource Justice:** We demand an end to the exploitative extraction of natural resources, particularly in Africa. Our goal is to champion sustainable development practices that prioritize environmental protection and equitable resource distribution.

8. **Eradicating Inequality and Discrimination:**
- **Equality for All:** Our vision is a world free from racism, sexism, and all forms of discrimination. We advocate for reforms in job applications and other systems to guarantee equal opportunities for all, regardless of skin color, gender, or any other arbitrary factor.

Our Vision for a Flourishing Future:

Beyond these immediate objectives, we strive towards a future where:
- **Peace prevails:** Conflicts are resolved through dialogue and diplomacy, not violence. Justice and fairness guide international relations.
- **Non-violence reigns:** We advocate for global reforms that prevent violence and promote peace, justice, and equality.
- **Global Constitutionalism:** We champion a universal

set of principles and laws governing international relations and domestic policies, fostering stability and cooperation.

- **International Solidarity:** We encourage nations to collaborate, rather than compete, in addressing global challenges.
- **Ethical Governance:** We demand transparency, accountability, and ethical leadership across all nations.
- **Global Scientific Collaboration:** We foster international cooperation in scientific research, sharing knowledge and technology to tackle global challenges and improve lives.
- **Digital Inclusion:** We advocate for universal access to affordable and reliable digital connectivity, ensuring everyone benefits from the digital age.
- **Peaceful Coexistence:** We promote dialogue and understanding among diverse cultures and religions, fostering a world where people of all backgrounds live together respectfully.
- **Sustainable Agriculture:** We champion practices that protect the environment, ensure food security, and empower rural communities.
- **Refugee Rights Upheld:** We advocate for the human dignity and basic rights of refugees and displaced persons, ensuring their safety and access to essential services.
- **Gender Equality Achieved:** We strive for equal opportunities and representation for women in all aspects of society, dismantling discriminatory practices and promoting female leadership.
- **Climate Action:** We demand urgent action to address the climate crisis, transitioning to renewable energy, adopting sustainable practices, and safeguarding our planet for future generations.
- **Artistic Expression Flourishes:** We support freedom of expression and artistic creativity, enriching our

collective human experience with the power of culture and art.
- **Animal Welfare Prioritized:** We advocate for the humane treatment of animals in all aspects of their lives.
- **Fair Global Trade:** We promote fair and equitable trade practices that benefit all nations, upholding human rights and environmental standards.
- **The Rule of Law Triumphs:** We uphold the rule of law at all levels, ensuring justice, human rights protection, and the eradication of corruption.
- **Responsible Media Empowered:** We encourage ethical journalism, combat misinformation, and ensure the media serves the public interest.
- **Innovation Drives Progress:** We foster a culture of innovation, supporting scientific research, technological advancements, and creative solutions to overcome challenges.

Conclusion:
Our unwavering commitment is to tirelessly work towards a world rooted in peace, justice, and equality. We believe these fundamental values are the bedrock of a brighter future for all. Our key objectives and demands serve as a roadmap for this collective endeavor. We invite all individuals, organizations, and nations to join hands and transform our world into a haven of harmony, prosperity, and shared well-being.

Our Missions, Concerns, and Demands

Our Guiding Vision: A World Without Conflict, Exploitation, or Inequality

Our organization is dedicated to realizing a world free from conflict, exploitation, and inequality. We believe in the power of collective action and advocate for the following key objectives and demands to achieve this vision:

Global Accessibility and Impact:
- **Global Distribution and Translation:** We demand the distribution of this book to all living former and current

presidents of nations worldwide, translated into every currently spoken language. This ensures its accessibility and impact on a global audience.
- **Active Global Engagement:** We strive to participate actively in key international forums like the United Nations, NATO, and future gatherings of the United Countries of the World. Our focus will be on issues pertinent to developing nations, ensuring their voices are heard and needs addressed.

Peaceful Conflict Resolution and Sustainable Development:
- **Ending Exploitation:** We demand an end to the systematic exploitation of natural resources, particularly in impoverished continents like Africa. We call for sustainable development practices that respect the environment and ensure equitable distribution of resources.
- **Peaceful Conflict Resolution:** We firmly believe in the power of reconciliation and peaceful dialogue to resolve conflicts. We advocate for the adoption of principles that promote peaceful resolutions and condemn the violent overthrow of legitimate governments through coups d'état.

A World Free from Discrimination and War:
- **A World Free from Wars and Racism:** We envision a world where wars are neither seen nor heard, and where systematic racism based on skin color and gender is eradicated. We advocate for reforms in job application processes to eliminate discriminatory practices and promote equal opportunities for all.

Our Demands for a Just and Equitable World:
While the translation of this book and the pursuit of peaceful conflict resolution are crucial, our demands extend further. We believe in a world where justice, equality, and sustainability prevail, and we advocate for the following:
- **Global Awareness:** We demand the translation of this book into all currently spoken languages, enhancing its

accessibility and impact on a global scale.
- **Conflict Resolution through Peace:** We emphasize that conflict resolution should be pursued solely through peaceful means, in line with the supreme laws of visionary constitutions across nations.
- **Active Global Engagement:** We strive to participate in key international forums, especially focusing on issues pertinent to developing nations.
- **Combating Exploitation:** We work towards halting the systematic exploitation of natural resources, particularly in impoverished continents like Africa.
- **Promotion of Systematic Equality:** We address the pervasive issue of systematic racism, advocating for reforms in job applications to eliminate discrimination based on race or gender.

Our Vision for a Peaceful and Equitable Future:
Our vision for the future is one where peace, justice, and equality prevail. We advocate for the following principles to guide our actions and shape the world we envision:
- **Vision for a Peaceful Future:** We dream of a world where conflicts are resolved through dialogue, not violence, and where the principles of justice and fairness prevail over aggression and exploitation.
- **Advocacy for Non-Violent Change:** We urge for reforms that prevent violence and promote peace, justice, and equality, globally.
- **Promotion of Global Constitutionalism:** We highlight the need for a universal set of principles and laws that govern international relations and domestic policies.
- **Call for International Solidarity:** We encourage nations and their leaders to work together in addressing global challenges, emphasizing cooperation over competition.
- **Demand for Ethical Governance:** We advocate for transparent, accountable, and ethical leadership across all nations.

Beyond Borders and Boundaries:
Our pursuit of a better future extends beyond traditional borders and boundaries. We believe in:
- **Global Collaboration in Science:** Fostering international cooperation in scientific research, promoting the sharing of knowledge and technology to address global challenges and improve the lives of all.
- **Digital Access:** Advocating for universal access to affordable and reliable digital connectivity, ensuring that everyone has the opportunity to participate in the digital age and benefit from its advancements.
- **Peaceful Coexistence:** Promoting dialogue and understanding among different cultures and religions, fostering a world where people of all backgrounds can coexist peacefully and respectfully.

Protecting Our Planet and People:
We stand for:
- **Sustainable Agriculture:** Supporting sustainable agricultural practices that protect the environment, ensure food security, and uplift rural communities.
- **Refugee Rights:** Standing up for the rights of refugees and displaced persons, emphasizing their human dignity and the need for safe haven and access to essential services.
- **Gender Equality:** Striving for gender equality in all facets of society, dismantling discriminatory practices and promoting women's empowerment and leadership.
- **Climate Action:** Taking urgent action to address the climate crisis, transitioning to renewable energy sources, promoting sustainable practices, and protecting our planet for future generations.

Empowering Creativity and Responsibility:
We believe in:
- **Artistic Expression:** Supporting freedom of expression and artistic creativity, fostering a world where culture and art can flourish.

Conclusion:

Our organization is unwavering in its commitment to building a world where peace, justice, and equality are not distant dreams but lived realities. We believe that these fundamental values are the cornerstones of a better future for all humanity. Our key objectives and demands, outlined in this chapter, are not merely aspirations; they are a call to action, a roadmap for collective transformation.

We urge individuals, organizations, and nations to join hands in this vital endeavor. Let us move beyond apathy and division, forging unity through shared purpose. Together, we can translate these demands into tangible actions, dismantling the structures of conflict, exploitation, and inequality.

Let this book serve as a beacon, illuminating the path towards a world where wars are replaced by dialogue, exploitation by fair distribution, and discrimination by inclusivity. Let us embrace the power of collective action and build a future where every individual can thrive in a world free from fear and injustice.

This is not just our mission; it is our shared responsibility. Let us work together, with unwavering determination, to create a world worthy of our shared humanity.

CHAPTER 35

BREAKING THE CHAINS: A MANIFESTO FOR AFRICAN SOVEREIGNTY AND GLOBAL JUSTICE

Rising Together: A Collaborative Path to a Prosperous Africa and a Peaceful World

A Call for Change: A Path to a Prosperous Africa and a Peaceful World

Introduction:

This chapter presents a series of **dynamic and collaborative proposals** that African leaders, alongside other global stakeholders, can undertake. These proposals aim to address the continent's long-standing challenges and create a brighter future for its people. They are designed to promote **peace, justice, and equality**, and to ensure that Africa's natural resources are **effectively and sustainably utilized** for the benefit of its people.

Actions for a Prosperous Africa and a Peaceful World:

9. **Collaborative Partnerships:** Instead of a complete withdrawal, African leaders should prioritize seeking **mutually beneficial partnerships** with foreign charities. These partnerships should focus on **empowering local communities** through capacity building and sustainable development initiatives.
10. **Awareness and Transparency:** African leaders must exhibit a commitment to **transparency and vigilance** regarding the activities of foreign organizations. Collaboration with civil society and international partners is essential to **distinguish between legitimate aid and exploitative practices**.
11. **Accountability and Justice:** A **unified African body** should hold both internal and external actors accountable for exploiting Africa's resources. This includes ensuring that there are **legal consequences for powerful nations** involved in unfair practices.
12. **Nurturing a Culture of Peace:** Instead of focusing solely on criminalizing war, it is crucial to emphasize **education, diplomacy, and addressing root causes** such as poverty and inequality in order to promote conflict resolution. Celebrating peaceful solutions to past conflicts is a positive step forward.
13. **Respectful Engagement:** Treating all nations with **dignity and equality**, regardless of their size or power, is essential. Encouraging global partners to **engage with African countries respectfully** and refrain from interference in their internal affairs is crucial for fostering meaningful relationships.

14. **Self-Reliance and Cooperation:** African nations should come together to **chart their own course** and effectively utilize their resources for the benefit of their people. International cooperation should be based on **mutual respect and shared goals**, rather than external directives.
15. **United but Diverse:** Aspiring to establish a **unified African entity** that embraces the continent's diverse interests and aspirations while honoring the unique identities and cultures of individual nations is essential.
16. **Solutions beyond Borders:** Supporting the formation of **non-political organizations and initiatives** that transcend national boundaries and focus on global cooperation and peacebuilding is key to addressing global challenges effectively.
17. **Global Resource Equity:** Striving for **equitable distribution of global resources** is vital to ensure that no continent or country is exploited for the benefit of others. Promoting **fair trade practices and sustainable resource management** is crucial in achieving this goal.
18. **Peaceful Sovereignty:** Calling for the **withdrawal of all foreign military forces** from African soil and other lands is a fundamental step in promoting sovereignty and self-determination for all nations.
19. **Dismantling Systemic Inequities:** Addressing systemic issues such as **modern colonization, exploitation, and discrimination** in all forms is paramount. Advocating for reforms that ensure **equal opportunities and empowerment for marginalized communities** is essential for social progress.

Conclusion: By implementing these **cooperative and forward-thinking actions**, African leaders, alongside the global community, can foster a **prosperous and peaceful future** not just for Africa, but for the entire world. This chapter serves as a **compelling call to action for unity, collaboration, and a shared vision of a just and equitable global society**.

Empowering a Global Community: A Blueprint for a Peaceful and Equitable Future

Preamble:

In an era of unprecedented global interconnectedness, we stand at a crossroads. We face a multitude of challenges that demand **collective action and innovative solutions**. This blueprint presents a comprehensive framework for a **global constitution** - a set of **guiding principles and enforceable mechanisms** that will form the foundation for a peaceful, equitable, and prosperous future for all.

Key Principles:

- **Supremacy of the Global Constitution:** The global constitution will take precedence over national laws, **ensuring global governance** and preventing any country from acting above its principles.
- **Enforceable Adherence:** An independent global court will **monitor and enforce compliance**, ensuring that all nations adhere to the established principles and imposing sanctions for violations.
- **Reformed United Nations:** Empowering the United Nations to **oversee implementation** and **coordinate global efforts** on pressing issues is vital for effective global governance.
- **Human Rights and Security:** Prioritizing **human safety and peace** by banning weapons of mass destruction, limiting firearms, and prohibiting war media is crucial for safeguarding human rights and fostering a secure environment.
- **Self-Determination and Non-interference:** Protecting the right to self-determination for all nations, including ending modern colonization and foreign intervention, is a core principle of the global constitution.

- **Social Justice and Equality:** Eradicating harmful practices such as forced labor, prostitution, and discrimination is essential for promoting **equal opportunities and dignity for all individuals**.
- **Global Cooperation and Accountability:** Establishing global leadership structures, accessible communication technologies, and ensuring free access to information will encourage **collaboration and shared responsibility** among nations.

Conclusion: This blueprint presents a bold vision that can be achieved through collective commitment and ongoing dialogue. It is not a rigid rulebook but a flexible framework that can adapt to the evolving needs of our world. By embracing the principles outlined here, we can build a future where:

- **Peace prevails:** Conflict is resolved through diplomacy, cooperation, and addressing root causes. Weapons of war are dismantled, and violence is not tolerated.
- **Justice flourishes:** Every individual, regardless of their origin, background, or beliefs, has equal rights and opportunities. Discrimination, exploitation, and oppression are eradicated.
- **Sustainability thrives:** We live in harmony with our planet, using resources responsibly and ensuring a healthy environment for generations to come.
- **Prosperity abounds:** Everyone has access to basic necessities, education, and opportunities to reach their full potential. Poverty and hunger are eliminated.
- **Innovation blossoms:** We harness the power of collaboration and knowledge sharing to solve global challenges and create a better future for all.

This is not just a dream; it is a choice. Each individual, each community, each nation can contribute to building this brighter future. Let us choose unity over division, cooperation over competition, and compassion over indifference. Let us write a new chapter in human history, one where the words "Empowering a Global Community" are not just a title, but a lived reality.

CHAPTER 36

THE TRANQUILITY MANIFESTO: CHOOSING THE RIGHT PATH TO PEACEFUL SLEEP

For a peaceful night's sleep every day, let us cultivate the habit of doing the right thing. Our conscience will serve as our unwavering compass as we navigate life's complexities. By committing to what's just, we pave the way for a lifetime of restful nights, where the satisfaction of righteous actions cradles us in inner peace.

To stay on this path of integrity, let us regularly revisit the principles outlined in this book. They serve as a star chart on our life's journey, empowering us to consistently make ethical choices.

In a world consumed by greed, relentless fame and power grabs, and the exploitation of less fortunate regions, choosing the right path can feel daunting. But let us remember to replace these destructive desires with a genuine yearning to do what's right. This shift in priorities won't just contribute to a better world, it will grant us the tranquility and restful sleep we deserve, night after night, in this fleeting life we call existence.

Cultivate Mindfulness:
For a life of tranquility, mindfulness is an indispensable tool. By being fully present in the moment, we can detach from the whirlwind of thoughts and worries that disrupt our peace.
Mindfulness isn't about suppressing thoughts or emotions; it's about observing them without judgment, letting them pass like clouds in the sky. This practice cultivates inner calm and resilience, enabling us to navigate life's challenges with grace.

Embrace Acceptance:
Acceptance is the foundation of a tranquil life. It's not about resignation or passivity; it's about acknowledging things as they are, without resistance or judgment.
Accepting the present moment, even when it's difficult, frees us from the burden of wishing it were different. It allows us to focus on what we can control, rather than dwelling on what we can't.

Practice Forgiveness:
Forgiveness is the ultimate act of self-compassion. It's not about condoning wrongdoing; it's about releasing ourselves from the shackles of anger, resentment, and bitterness.
Forgiveness doesn't mean forgetting; it means letting go of the emotional baggage that weighs us down. It allows us to move forward with a lighter heart and a clearer mind.

Nurture Gratitude:
Gratitude is the antidote to negativity and fear. It shifts our focus from what we lack to what we already have, cultivating a sense of abundance and contentment.
Taking time to appreciate the simple joys of life – the sun's warmth, nature's beauty, the love of our loved ones – fills our hearts with gratitude. This positive energy radiates outwards,

creating a more harmonious and peaceful existence.

Live with Integrity:
Living with integrity means aligning our thoughts, words, and actions with our values. It's about being true to ourselves, even when it's difficult.

Integrity fosters a sense of inner peace and self-respect. It allows us to sleep soundly at night, knowing we've lived a life of authenticity and purpose.

Conclusion:
A life of tranquility is not a passive state of being; it is an active choice, a conscious commitment to cultivate inner peace and harmony. It's about aligning our thoughts, actions, and values to create a life that resonates with our authentic selves.

The principles outlined in this book, coupled with consistent practice and dedication, can guide us towards a life of tranquility and peaceful slumber. Let us embrace mindfulness, acceptance, forgiveness, gratitude, and integrity as the cornerstones of our journey.

As we embark on this path, let us remember that tranquility is not a destination; it is a continuous practice, a way of being that evolves with each passing moment. Let us embrace the challenges and imperfections along the way, for they are opportunities for growth and self-discovery.

Just Do the Right Thing: A Path to Tranquility and Peaceful Sleep
For a life bathed in the moonlight of tranquility and cradled by the lullaby of peaceful sleep, let us cultivate the habit of doing the right thing. Let our conscience be our compass, guiding us through life's labyrinthine alleys and pointing us towards the open fields of ethical clarity. Each righteous choice, like a seed sown in fertile soil, blossoms into a night of restful slumber, where the satisfaction of integrity soothes our souls.

To remain on this sunlit path, let us frequently reflect upon the principles laid bare in these pages. They will serve as our anchor in turbulent seas, equipping us to navigate ethical dilemmas with clarity and purpose. In a world often consumed by avarice, the relentless pursuit of hollow crowns, and the exploitation of vulnerable lands, choosing the right path can feel like scaling a sheer cliff face. Yet, let us replace these destructive desires with a yearning, as deep as the roots of ancient trees, to do what is right. This recalibration of values, this shift from shadows to sunlight, will not only ripple outwards, contributing to a more just and equitable world, but will also grant us the tranquility and restful sleep we deserve, night after night, in this fleeting symphony of existence we call life.

Cultivate Mindfulness

To cultivate a life of tranquility, mindfulness is our indispensable tool. By being fully present in the moment, we can disentangle ourselves from the maelstrom of anxieties that often disrupt our peace. Mindfulness is not about stifling thoughts or emotions; it's like watching a wisp of smoke dance in the wind – observe them without judgment, allow them to pass, and return to the stillness of the present. This practice, honed with time, cultivates inner calm and resilience, enabling us to navigate life's challenges with the composure of a mountain standing tall against the wind.

Embrace Acceptance

Acceptance is the foundation of a tranquil life. It is not acquiescence or apathy; it is acknowledging that things are the way they are, without resistance or the emotional weight of longing for what cannot be. Accepting the present moment, even when it's clothed in thorns, frees us from the burden of wishing things were different. It allows us to focus on what we can control, like tending to the garden of our own being, rather than dwelling on what lies beyond our reach.

Practice Forgiveness

Forgiveness is the ultimate act of self-compassion. It is not about condoning wrongdoing; it is about releasing ourselves from the psychological shackles of anger, resentment, and bitterness. Forgiveness doesn't mean forgetting; it means letting go of the emotional baggage that weighs us down. It allows us to move forward with a lighter heart, unburdened by the ghosts of the past, and a clearer mind to create a brighter future.

Nurture Gratitude
Gratitude is the antidote to negativity and fear. It shifts our focus from the shadows of what we lack to the sunlit fields of what we already possess, cultivating a sense of abundance and contentment. Take time to appreciate the simple pleasures of life – the warmth of sunlight on your skin, the laughter of loved ones, the silent symphony of nature – and let gratitude fill your heart like a bursting dam. This positive energy, like a ripple of positivity, expands into the world around you, creating a more harmonious and peaceful existence for yourself and those around you.

Live with Integrity
Living with integrity means aligning our thoughts, words, and actions with the north star of our values. It is about being true to ourselves, even when it's difficult, even when the path seems treacherous. Integrity fosters a sense of inner peace and self-respect. It allows us to sleep soundly at night, knowing that we have lived a life of authenticity and purpose, a life that resonates with our truest selves.

By embodying these principles, by weaving them into the fabric of our being, we transform our lives into a journey of tranquility and peaceful slumber.

Conclusion:
A life of tranquility is not a state of inertia; it is an active choice, a deliberate dedication to cultivating inner peace and harmony. It is about aligning our thoughts, actions, and values to create a life that sings in tune with our authentic selves. The principles outlined in this book, coupled with consistent practice and unwavering dedication, can serve as our guiding stars on our path to tranquility and peaceful sleep. Let us embrace mindfulness, acceptance, forgiveness, gratitude, and integrity as the cornerstones of our journey.

Remember, tranquility is not a destination; it is a continuous practice, a way of being that evolves with each passing breath. Let us embrace the challenges and imperfections along the way, for they are opportunities for growth and self-discovery. As we

walk this path, let us remember that we are not alone. We are a part of a vast tapestry of beings, all yearning for peace.
Not just for ourselves, but for the generations yet to come.
Let us be the architects of a world bathed in moonlight, where restful sleep is not a luxury, but a birthright. Let the ripple of our individual choices become a wave of positive change, washing away the darkness and ushering in a dawn of collective peace.
Start small. Choose honesty in a world filled with deceit. Offer compassion where there is only judgment. Forgive yourself, forgive others, and let go of the burdens that weigh you down. Nurture gratitude for the simple miracles that surround you, and let it blossom into a radiant light that warms your soul and illuminates the path for others.
Remember, every right action, every choice made with integrity, is a pebble tossed into the pond. Together, these ripples will become a tidal wave of change, transforming not just your life, but the world around you. So, go forth, do the right thing, and sleep soundly, knowing that you are building a symphony of tranquility, one note at a time.
May your dreams be filled with stars, and your nights cradled by the gentle lullaby of a world at peace.
In the quietude of peaceful nights, may we find the courage to continue choosing the right thing, knowing that each choice, like a pebble tossed into a still pond, creates ripples of positive change that reach far beyond the horizon of our own lives. May we find solace in the knowledge that we are not alone on this path, but are joined by countless others who yearn for a world bathed in the moonlight of tranquility. Together, let us build this world, brick by brick, choice by choice, breath by breath.

The Tranquility Manifesto: Choosing the Right Path to Peaceful Sleep
Sleep Soundly, Live Rightly: A Guide to Inner Peace in a Chaotic World
Unshackled Slumber: Cultivating Tranquility Through Righteous Choices
The Right Stuff for Restful Nights: A Blueprint for Ethical

Living and Peaceful Sleep
Whispers of the Soul: How Doing the Right Thing Lulls You into Tranquil Sleep
A Call to Action:

undefined

A Resonant Image:

undefined

A Personal Connection:

undefined

A Provocative Question:

undefined

A Moment of Gratitude:

undefined

CHAPTER 37

ECHOES OF RESISTANCE: TWO NATIONS, ONE DREAM OF FREEDOM

Shared Threads of Freedom: The American and Eritrean Struggles

Introduction:

The American and Eritrean peoples are connected by a remarkable tapestry of history, characterized by unwavering courage, resilience, and an unyielding pursuit of freedom. Despite the vast oceans that separate them, their struggles against seemingly insurmountable odds unite them in a common journey towards justice. These parallel narratives, though unique in their details, resonate with powerful similarities, reflecting the universal human desire for self-determination and the belief in a just world.

The American Revolution: A Cry for Liberty

In the face of British rule and longing for the ideals of freedom and self-governance enshrined in Enlightenment thought, the American colonists rose up to ignite a revolution that would shape history forever. Patriots such as George Washington and Benjamin Franklin, driven by their unwavering belief in liberty, confronted tyranny with both weapons and words. The battles of Lexington and Concord echoed the colonists' resounding call for freedom, and after eight arduous years, the United States of America emerged as a beacon of hope for oppressed people across the globe.

The Eritrean Struggle: Defiance Against Injustice

In the Horn of Africa, the Eritrean people embarked on a similar quest for liberation, their spirit hardened by centuries of subjugation under Ethiopian emperors. Facing the harsh rule of Haile Selassie and Mengistu Hailemariam, the Eritreans refused to be silenced. United under the Eritrean People's Liberation Front (EPLF), a guerrilla force forged in the crucible of hardship, they employed unconventional tactics such as lightning attacks and demonstrated unwavering unity in the face of great sacrifice. Ultimately, their relentless determination led to the dawn of Eritrean independence in 1991.

Shared Threads, Universal Truths:

These parallel narratives, though separated by time and distance, resonate with a profound truth: the human spirit, kindled by the fires of injustice, burns with an indomitable flame. Regardless of the oppressor or the chains that bind, the yearning for freedom and the pursuit of a just society course through the veins of humanity.

A Timeless Struggle: Liberty versus Oppression

The struggles of America and Eritrea are not mere relics of the past; they embody the timeless battle between the forces of liberty and oppression. From ancient Athens defying Persian tyranny to Nelson Mandela's fight against apartheid in South Africa, history is replete with stories of collective will triumphing over seemingly insurmountable odds. These struggles serve as powerful reminders that even the mightiest empires crumble when faced with the unwavering resolve of a united people fighting for freedom.

A Future of Hope: Shattering the Chains

The echoes of these victories reverberate into the future, offering hope to oppressed communities around the world. From the ongoing fight for democracy in Myanmar to the tireless resistance against authoritarian regimes, the spirit of liberty, ignited by the struggles of America and Eritrea, continues to inspire. We stand at the precipice of a future where the shackles of tyranny will be shattered, and the voices of freedom and self-determination will resound without fear.

The Enduring Legacy: A Tapestry of Freedom

The struggles of America and Eritrea for freedom are not mere triumphs of the past; they are living legacies woven into the fabric of our present. The ideals of self-determination, enshrined in the American Declaration of Independence and the Eritrean Constitution, continue to guide our societies. The sacrifices of countless heroes, from Nathan Hale to Kidane Gebrehiwot, serve as eternal reminders of the price of liberty and the responsibility we bear to safeguard it.

Conclusion:

The shared tapestry of freedom, woven with the threads of the American and Eritrean struggles, stands as a powerful testament to the enduring human spirit and the unwavering pursuit of justice. Their stories offer not just a glimpse into the past, but a torch illuminating the path towards a future where liberty reigns supreme. Let us carry their legacy, fueled by their courage and guided by their unwavering belief, as we strive to build a world where the voices of freedom forever echo in glorious harmony.

CHAPTER 38

VISIONS FOR A PEACEFUL TOMORROW: REFLECTIONS ON SUCCESS, GLOBAL DYNAMICS, AND HUMANITARIAN PRINCIPLES

Cultivating Success as a Habit
"The seed of success is planted with the first instance of achievement, growing into a habit with continuous nurturing. The core ingredient is problem-solving, no matter the scale.

All successful individuals embody this trait. The formula for success involves unwavering focus, shunning distractions, and implementing robust timelines for mitigating issues. The breadth of your success directly corresponds to the scope of the problems you confront. Overcoming personal obstacles gives rise to individual victories, while addressing global concerns like World Wars can herald historical triumphs of unparalleled magnitude. By adhering to these principles of success, challenges of any dimension can be surmounted."

The Intricacies of Sanctions and Invasions
"Levying sanctions on nations escalates to an extreme variant of global authoritarianism, a phenomenon unseen in modern annals. The deepest wounds inflicted by sanctions are born not by governments but by innocent civilians. The pressing concern is to identify the real victims of sanctions, invariably the innocents, leading us to understand that sanctions often wreak more havoc than they mend.
Invasions of sovereign territories epitomize the zenith of autocratic acts, delivering the harshest blows to always the innocent residents, making such incursions more damaging than beneficial."

The Ordinary Citizen's Role in Sustaining Peace
"Neither sanctions nor invasions carve a route towards lasting peace; they merely perpetuate cycles of conflict and unease. Genuine peace unfolds in an environment stripped of such aggressive maneuvers, a place where tranquility and collaboration can sprout and bloom for generations to come."

The Philosophy of Dr. Wisdom Zerit Teklay
"Dr. Wisdom Zerit Teklay, a pioneering champion of peace and well-being, presides over Amazoxa Peace University, leaving a substantial footprint in Zerit-Tonianism Philosophy and Nutrition. His teachings resonate with the call for wisdom, justice, equality, and ubiquitous health. He envisions a world where the law's hand reaches everyone, even those in power,

advocating for integrity on every societal rung. His philosophy lights the path towards a more equitable and peaceful global community."

Additional Reflections

- State-implemented torture, especially targeted at innocents, starkly infringes upon human rights and demands immediate worldwide denunciation and elimination.
- The practice of overclassification often veils truths under the guise of national security demands. A fine balance between transparency and the necessary secrecy must be struck.
- A definitive justice system should serve as a shield for the marginalized and innocent, far removed from being an instrument of oppression.
- Self-care holds paramount importance in the upkeep of our mental and physical health, enabling us to contribute more fruitfully to societal betterment.
- The prospect of World War demands a unified, global response, extending beyond governments to include every citizen. By advocating for peace and diplomatic resolutions in our daily engagements, we each play a crucial role in averting global discord.
- The standards of non-aggression and respect we demand from media should be echoed in our online behavior, fostering a digital environment of peace and mutual respect.
- In summation, the preservation of peace is a shared effort, reaching beyond governmental bodies to each individual. Upholding the pillars of wisdom, justice, equality, and health steers us towards a world devoid of violence and conflict. Outspoken opposition to inhumane practices, insisting on transparency, and advocating for a fair justice system are critical steps towards realizing this vision. Self-care equips us to be more potent agents of peace and diplomacy, leading us towards a global community where the prospect of World War becomes an obsolete notion, supplanted by a society rooted in harmony and mutual respect."

Conclusion: A Roadmap towards a Just and Harmonious World

In conclusion, the pathway to a world defined by harmony, justice, and enduring peace is not a solitary one. It begins with the individual, transmuting success into an everyday habit rooted in effective problem-solving. While global issues like sanctions and invasions often seem outside the control of the individual, we must recognize their profound impact on the innocent and commit to fostering dialogue and understanding instead.

The part played by everyday citizens in this context is pivotal. Through active participation, advocacy, and a relentless pursuit of peaceful solutions, each one of us can significantly influence the narrative of national and global politics, guiding humanity away from aggression and towards understanding and negotiations.

Dr. Wisdom Zerit Teklay's philosophy illuminates this path, underscoring wisdom, justice, equality, and health's significance. His ethos serves as a beacon, guiding us towards a world where ethical conduct and accountability are universally practiced, transcending societal levels.

Simultaneously, our collective conscience must stand firm against practices that undermine human dignity and rights, such as torture and opaque governance. Demanding a transparent, fair, and just legal system is not just essential; it's non-negotiable in upholding the rights and dignity of all individuals, particularly the marginalized and voiceless.

On the flip side, nurturing our own physical and mental well-being through self-care practices equips us to contribute more effectively to the societal fabric. This harmonious balancing act extends to our digital lives, fostering respect and understanding amidst the often polarized online world.

Lastly, the vision of a world free from the threat of conflict on a scale as massive as World War is not a utopian dream but an achievable reality. It calls for a united effort that transcends governments, encompassing every individual's contributions. By harnessing the pillars of wisdom, justice, equality, and health, we can reshape our global community into one where conflict and aggression are relics of the past, replaced by the emblems of peace, cooperation, and mutual understanding.

CHAPTER 39

GLOBAL HARMONY REDEFINED: THE WISDOMATIC VISION OF DR. WISDOM ZERIT TEKLAY

Dr. Wisdom Zerit Teklay, the visionary behind Wisdom 101 and the founder of the Wisdom World People Party, presents a compelling vision for a world united in wisdom and peace. Challenging traditional notions of nationality and identity, he puts forth a modern philosophy that transcends boundaries and promotes unity.

Addressing the issue of birth certificates, Dr. Wisdom Zerit Teklay takes a critical look at their role in perpetuating discrimination. He proposes an innovative approach that redefines the concept of birthplace, potentially leading to a significant reduction in global racism.

Known for his groundbreaking work in Wisdomatic Natural Medicine and Wholesome Wisdomatic Natural Psychology, Dr. Wisdom Zerit Teklay is a staunch advocate for human intelligence. He believes in the power of human intellect and calls for global independence and unity, asserting the superiority of human intelligence over artificial intelligence.

In his political aspirations, Dr. Wisdom Teklay transcends traditional party lines. He seeks the presidency of both the United States and Eritrea, focusing on the values of global unity, peace, and opposing covert operations and dictatorships.

Dr. Wisdom Zerit Teklay's philosophy revolves around the principles of wisdom, justice, equality, and good health. He envisions a world where no person, including government officials, is above the law. His philosophy is a call for universal accountability and obedience to the principles of justice.

Strongly condemning government-sponsored torture, Dr. Wisdom Zerit Teklay emphasizes the inhumanity of such acts and calls for their immediate cessation. His unwavering stance against torture reflects his commitment to justice and human rights.

Questioning the need for highly classified information, Dr. Wisdom Zerit Teklay advocates for transparency in government actions. He believes that excessive classification often does more harm than good to society, and calls for a more open and accountable governing system.

Criticizing the justice system, Dr. Wisdom Zerit Teklay highlights its failure to protect the poor and marginalized. He argues that the system often favors the wealthy who can afford powerful lawyers, perpetuating inequality. His critique aims to bring attention to the flaws within the system and calls for reform.

Recognizing the importance of self-care, Dr. Wisdom Zerit Teklay emphasizes its role in maintaining mental and physical health. He believes that personal well-being is essential not only for individuals but also for the welfare of society as a whole.

Addressing the threat of World War, Dr. Wisdom Zerit Teklay calls for collective responsibility in preventing such global conflicts. He advocates for diplomacy and peace, rejecting the idea of superpower competition, and proposing global equality as a solution.

Dr. Wisdom Zerit Teklay's health philosophy promotes a plant-based diet, avoiding processed foods and pharmaceuticals. He attributes his own good health to this lifestyle and actively advocates for natural medicine and psychology.

In his critique of artificial intelligence, Dr. Wisdom Zerit Teklay highlights the limitations of AI compared to the boundless capabilities of human intelligence. His argument draws attention to the potential drawbacks of excessive reliance on artificial intelligence.

Driven by his global vision, Dr. Wisdom Teklay actively promotes peace, justice, and equality. He envisions a world where conflicts are resolved through wisdom and understanding, rather than through force and aggression.

In conclusion, Dr. Wisdom Zerit Teklay's manifesto for global leadership and cooperation invites readers to join him in creating a unified world guided by wisdom, peace, and understanding. His ideas offer hope for a more harmonious and just future.

CHAPTER 40

DR. WISDOM ZERIT TEKLAY: BEYOND BORDERS, BEYOND LIMITS

Dr. Wisdom Zerit Teklay: A Citizen of the World and Catalyst for Progress

Visionary, thinker, and influential figure: Dr. Teklay's proficiency extends across a range of unique fields:

- **Wisdom 101:** A revolutionary method for unleashing personal and collective wisdom.
- **Contemporary Birth Certificate Philosophy:** Contesting outdated perceptions of identity and belonging.
- **Inspirational Organic Comedy:** Fusing humour with insightful societal commentary for constructive influence.
- **World's Got Talent (WGT):** Advocating for unbounded

creative expression on a worldwide scale.
- **World Independence Day (September 30th):** Ushering the notions of universal unity and liberty into prominence.

Founder and President of the Wisdom World People Party (WWPP): Dr. Teklay passionately champions inclusion and global citizenship, setting an example through his actions.

Author of "Wisdom 101": His insightful wisdom emboldens world leaders and individuals alike.

Reimagining the Birth Certificate: Dr. Teklay courageously critiques the shortcomings of customary birth certificates:
- Perpetuating bias and discrimination based on an individual's birthplace.
- Ignoring a person's inherent wisdom and limitless potential.
- Neglecting the deeper aspects of identity by focusing solely on birthplace, name, and date.

Proposed Solution: Boldly, Dr. Teklay updates his own birthplace to "The World," inspiring individuals to:
- Embrace their global identity, shattering geographical borders.
- Recognize their inherent wisdom and unique contributions to the world.
- Select their sense of belonging, irrespective of their birthplace.

Adopting Global Citizenship: Dr. Teklay stands as a candidate for President of any nation, staunchly believing that:
- Leadership should transcend nationality, focusing on merit and shared values.
- Wisdom and inclusivity can shape a brighter, more inclusive future for all.
- The WWPP's message of global citizenship bridges people across nations and cultures.

World Independence Day: Dr. Teklay fervently endorses September 30th as a day for the whole world to celebrate:
- Freedom from the constraints of bias and prejudice.

- Acknowledging our shared human journey and interconnectedness.
- Creating a fair and equitable world through combined efforts.

Dr. Teklay's message echoes globally: We are all citizens of the world, bound by our innate potential for wisdom and progress. Let's unite toward building a future where everyone feels acknowledged, valued, and empowered to offer their unique capabilities.

Greetings to all!

I am Dr. Wisdom Zerit Teklay, better known as Dr. Wisdom, an advocate for Wisdomatic Natural medicine and Wholesome Wisdomatic Natural Psychology.

I want to emphasize that I prioritize people over political affiliations. I am not aligned with any individual person, I focus on serving the people, acting as their voice.

I am a firm believer in human intelligence and authentic wisdom, often overshadowed by artificial intelligence.

As the originator of Inspirational Organic Comedy and Wisdom 101, I am pledged to disseminating knowledge and wisdom to world leaders, empowering them to enact positive changes.

Additionally, I take immense pride in declaring myself the founder of September 30 African Independence Day and September 30 World Independence Day, marking significant points in our historical timeline.

Moving on to my political party, the Wisdom People Party. I am pursuing the presidency of the United States, not bound by my birth certificate. You may find my candidacy for the President of the United States on the official Federal Election Commission's website at fec.gov or via a "Wisdom People Party" Google search.

I assure you that my focus extends past any politician or government. I am not tied to a particular political party, as I represent the Wisdom World People Party.

My ultimate aim entails fostering unity and cohesion for world peace. I am staunchly against any form of division that threatens global harmony.

I focus on the prosperity and well-being of all individuals, regardless of their nationality or background, rather than being pro or anti any individual.

Our focus should extend beyond political figures, centering on the wholesome people of various nations. For instance, I am pro the wholesome people of Russia, Ukraine, China, and Eritrea, my birthplace.

I staunchly advocate for fair and transparent elections. If elected as the President of Eritrea, I will serve as the youngest president, committed to preserving the sovereignty of the country and preventing foreign interference.

Covert Operation Cu Dieta, operating without the consensus of the wholesome people, embodies dictatorial terrorism. I stand against such covert operations, emphasizing the importance of the people's voice.

When it comes to conflicts and leaders, I prioritize the wholesome people. For example, I stand with the wholesome people of Eritrea, United States, Tigray, Ethiopia, Libya, Iraq, NATO and Non-NATO countries.

I want to reiterate that my focus isn't on countries or specific presidents, but rather on the wholesome people of the world, who rightfully deserve our attention and support.

Thank you for your time, and let's collaborate towards a brighter future for everyone.

CHAPTER 41

BEYOND ROASTING: THE POWER OF INCLUSIVE HUMOR IN INTERNATIONAL ORGANIC COMEDY

Amazoxa Peace University's INTERNATIONAL ORGANIC COMEDY is a unique and transformative form of entertainment that places emphasis on inclusivity and positivity. Unlike traditional comedy, Organic Comedy stands apart by refraining from making fun of individuals or engaging in roasting. It is a comedy form that staunchly upholds the values of respect and inclusiveness.

Organic Comedy is a powerful antidote to discrimination, and it categorically rejects any form of humor that is derived from age, race, gender, or any other characteristic. Moreover, it adamantly discourages violence, never endorsing war or horror movies.

By design, Organic Comedy is focused on self-expression rather than seeking validation. It provides a platform for comedians to share their unique perspectives and personal experiences without resorting to harmful or offensive content. The goal is to foster a greater understanding and empathy among audiences.

A shining example of the principles of Organic Comedy can be seen in Chris Rock's response when Will Smith playfully slapped him. Rather than reacting with anger or violence, Chris responded in a humorous and non-violent manner, remarking, "Wow, Will Smith just smacked the [expletive] out of me." This showcases the power of non-violent reaction and the ability to find humor even in unexpected situations.

In recognition of outstanding contributions to the realm of Organic Comedy, Amazoxa Peace University will be hosting the prestigious Dr. Wisdom Organic Comedy Award ceremony on September 30, 2024, at Cafe Coco, the birthplace of Organic Comedy on September 30, 2023. One of the distinguished recipients of this esteemed award will be Chris Rock, a true trailblazer in the field.

In addition to honoring exceptional comedians, Amazoxa Peace University extends its deepest appreciation to all the comedians who have brought laughter and joy into our lives. Their impact extends beyond mere amusement, as they inspire us to be more open, to express our truths fearlessly, and to share our opinions through the practice of Organic Freedom.

The role of comedians in society cannot be overstated. They play a crucial role in shedding light on social issues such as injustice, inequality, racism, and abuses of power by governments. Their courage and willingness to confront these challenges head-on serve as a powerful reminder for all of us not to remain complacent.

As a tribute to these remarkable individuals, I invite you to stand up and applaud for at least 60 seconds or more, honoring yourself, Dr. Wisdom Zerit, and all the comedians past and present. Together, let us celebrate the guardians of laughter and champions of a brighter world.

Chapter 42

IN THE DISTRICT OF COLUMBIA DISTRICT COURT
Dr. Wisdom Zerit Teklay
1624 Hermitage Park Drive
Hermitage, Tennessee 37076
United States of America
+1 615 970 1832
zeritprrcw@gmail.com
Pro Se Plaintiff

Dr. Wisdom Zerit Teklay
v.
District of Columbia District Court

MOTION FOR PERMISSION TO E-FILE

COME NOW, Plaintiff, Dr. Wisdom Zerit Teklay ("Movant"), by and through Pro Se, and hereby moves for an order granting

Movant permission to electronically file documents in this case.

In support of this motion, Movant states as follows:

Movant seeks to electronically file documents in this case for the following compelling reasons:

Experience improved efficiency and timeliness of filing, ensuring swift and accurate submission of documents.

Make a significant contribution to reducing our environmental impact by eliminating the need for paper filings, aligning with modern sustainability practices.

Realize substantial cost reduction associated with paper-based filing, allowing for the efficient allocation of resources.

Ensure enhanced accessibility to court records for all relevant parties, facilitating transparency and easy retrieval of information.

Movant has diligently familiarized themselves with the Local Rules of this Court and fully understands the procedures for e-filing. Movant is fully prepared to comply with all applicable requirements for e-filing, including the proficient use of the Court's Electronic Case Filing System (ECF).

Granting Movant's motion will greatly benefit both the esteemed Court and the Movant by streamlining the filing process and significantly reducing the administrative burden on the Court.

THEREFORE, Movant respectfully requests that this Court enter an order granting Movant permission to electronically file documents in this case.

Dated: Wednesday, December 6, 2023

Respectfully submitted,

Dr. Wisdom Zerit Teklay

CERTIFICATE OF SERVICE

I hereby certify that on this Wednesday, December 6, 2023, a true and correct copy of the foregoing Motion for Permission to E-File was served on all parties of record via Email and mail to the following addresses:

DISTRICT OF COLUMBIA DISTRICT COURT
333 Constitution Avenue, NW
Washington, DC 20001
dcd_intake@dcd.uscourts.gov

Dr. Wisdom Zerit Teklay

Dr. Wisdom Zerit is a Pro Se Eritrean-American polymath philosopher of Zerit-Tonianism philosophy, author, politician, and President of Amazoxa Peace University.

CLERK'S OFFICE OF DR.WISDOM ZERIT TEKLAY

President of Amazoxa Peace University
President of Wisdom People Party
Office Number: +1(615)-970-1832
Email   : zeritprrcw@gmail.com
Dr. Wisdom Author Page:

https://www.amazon.com/author/drzerit

Petition:
https://www.change.org/AbolishTheNaturalBornRequirment

o experience his enlightening perspective and profound wisdom, you may visit his YouTube channel:

https://www.youtube.com/@drwisdomforpresidentÂ

For further insight into his entrepreneurial endeavors, visit his business page at:Â

https://g.co/kgs/9vY3aj

https://wa.me/message/MHFABY26GTQUF1

CHAPTER 43

WISDOM 101: THE PATH TO GLOBAL PEACE THROUGH ZERIT-TONIANISM

Have you ever paused to reflect on the tremendous importance of global peace? If you share this deep concern for the well-being of our world, then this book is tailor-made for you. It is specifically crafted to resonate with individuals who genuinely care about fostering global harmony.
The esteemed author of this book is none other than Dr. Wisdom Zerit Teklay—an extraordinary philosopher hailing from Entrean America. Dr. Teklay is renowned for his groundbreaking Zerit-Tonianism philosophy and his expertise in Zenit-Tonian Nutrition. His unwavering dedication to the cause of world peace is truly remarkable.
Every year, on September 30th, the Wisdom World People Party conference convenes, attracting world leaders from various

nations including the United States of America, Canada, and the Commonwealth of the Bahamas. This influential gathering serves as a platform for reconciliation and unity, spearheaded by Dr. Teklay himself.

Prepare to be amazed by Wisdom 101, a revolutionary institution poised to redefine education as we know it. Under the visionary guidance of Project A1, followed by Project B1, Wisdom 101 aims to create a world characterized by enduring peace and unwavering justice.

Wisdom 101 firmly believes that wisdom is the pinnacle of education, and achieving wisdom is the highest form of success. Embracing the notion that self-care and autonomy go hand in hand, Wisdom 101 encourages individuals to become their own doctors—an empowering and transformative process. By championing peace over war, we strive to cultivate an environment of harmony, justice, equality, and optimal well-being for all.

May the Zerit-Tonianism philosophy be showered with blessings, and may Wisdom 101 and the entire world prosper as a result. Dedication to equality, justice, and good health for all lies at the very core of Wisdom 101's mission. Dr. Wisdom Zerit Teklay, an Eritrean-American philosopher, stands as the embodiment of peace and serves as the guiding light for Wisdom 101—Zerit-Tonianism philosophy's finest advocate.

CHAPTER 44

AMAZOXA PEACE UNIVERSITY: WHERE WISDOM IGNITES TRANSFORMATION AND HOPE

Building a Brighter Future Through
Education, Justice, and Harmony

Amazoxa Peace University presents a pioneering approach to education founded on Dr. Wisdom Zerit Teklay's visionary philosophy, Zerit-Tonianism. As a nascent institution conceived by this esteemed intellectual, our university imparts transformative learning centered on the principles of wisdom, justice, and human dignity.

Through the lens of Zerit-Tonianism, Dr. Teklay transcends conventional educational boundaries by emphasizing the pursuit of unadulterated knowledge and its potential for positive impact. Our university breathes life into this philosophy, establishing an intellectual haven committed to:
- Promoting global harmony by fostering connections between diverse cultures and communities.
- Upholding justice as the cornerstone of personal and societal interactions.
- Empowering individuals from all backgrounds to reach their full potential.
- Cultivating holistic well-being, encompassing mental, physical, and spiritual health.

As the tangible manifestation of Dr. Teklay's enduring legacy, Amazoxa Peace University offers more than academic degrees or credentials. We serve as a gateway to intellectual and personal transformation, guiding students to access their inner wisdom and ignite positive change.

Our approach affords students an enriched educational journey, enabling them to:
- Engage with Dr. Teklay's extensive writings and delve into the frontiers of Zerit-Tonian thought.
- Participate in cultural exchanges to foster intercultural understanding across borders.
- Develop leadership competencies to drive change on issues of equality, justice, and harmony.
- Nurture holistic wellness practices for self-care and inner peace.

By intertwining philosophy, culture, and personal growth, our university equips students with the wisdom, empathy, and purpose to navigate life's intricate pathways.

In his esteemed role as President of Amazoxa Peace University, Dr. Wisdom Teklay exemplifies a legacy that extends beyond the realm of academia. He fosters true education, nurturing generations to build a more just and harmonious world. His unwavering commitment to a people-centric ethos resonates worldwide, inspiring hope for a brighter future.

Plunge into the depths of Dr. Wisdom Zerit Teklay's profound insights and emerge empowered. This book extends an invitation to join a movement, to redefine the essence of knowledge and leadership, and to become a driving force for positive change.

Connect with a Visionary:

Embrace the World of Why Wisdom!

Dr. Wisdom's profound insights and transformative leadership extend beyond the pages of this book. Explore the depths of his wisdom and engage with his inspiring journey:

Delve into Dr. Wisdom's captivating writings: https://www.amazon.com/author/drzerit

Witness the unfolding brilliance on YouTube: @drwisdomforpresident ����

Replace plan contentRegenerate

CHAPTER 45

"Celebrating Progress: A New Year of Inclusive Leadership"

Breaking Barriers, Building Futures: The Wisdom People Party's Revolution for Inclusive Leadership

As the new year unfolds, we stand at the forefront of an era defined by inclusivity and equality. The Wisdom People Party proudly declares January 1st as an official holiday, heralding a new epoch—a nonviolent revolution aimed at eliminating the U.S. Presidency's natural-born citizen eligibility requirement. This movement, reminiscent of the monumental shift caused by the abolition of slavery, symbolizes transformative change.

Championed by Dr. Wisdom Zerit Teklay, this campaign represents more than an ideological shift; it is a vigorous, just demand. Celebrated annually, this day is a time for passion and introspection, symbolizing our steadfast, peaceful opposition to antiquated barriers in leadership.

Under Dr. Teklay's visionary guidance, the Wisdom People Party annually commemorates this day to honor a political milestone and the resilient spirit of a populace committed to enduring change. As we joyfully greet the new year and observe our official holiday, we also welcome a new era of leadership, unbound by the constraints of birthright and geography. This landmark achievement breathes new life into our collective journey.

Strengthened by this success, we advocate for a leadership model that reflects our nation's diversity. The abolition of the natural-born citizen requirement shines as a beacon of hope, heralding a progressive future where the highest office is accessible to all exceptionally qualified individuals, regardless of their place of birth.

As we embark on this new year and solemnly celebrate our official holiday, the significance of this monumental victory resonates within us. Our celebrations transcend traditional festivities; they embody our ongoing commitment to fostering a more inclusive, equitable, and representative society.

Happy New Year, and here's to our unwavering, nonviolent crusade for a more inclusive America. We express our deep gratitude to everyone who supports this cause. Your steadfast belief in our mission is the cornerstone of our persistent efforts to achieve a democracy that truly represents and serves justice. United by our diverse backgrounds and shared aspirations, we envision a future where leadership is determined by capability and vision, not origin. Each January 1st, henceforth, not only symbolizes our collective progress but also underscores the sustained effort required to realize our goals.

Empower America's Finest to Lead: Abolish the Outdated Natural-Born Citizen Requirement

Subject: Stand with Dr. Wisdom Zerit Teklay and Shape a Brighter Future for All

Dear Fellow Citizens,

At the core of American democracy lies a contradiction: we pride ourselves on being a nation of equal opportunity, yet our Constitution maintains an outdated, discriminatory barrier that prevents exceptional individuals from serving at the highest level. Today, we, the Concerned Citizens for Constitutional Equality, call for an amendment to abolish the archaic "natural-born citizen" requirement, an anachronism that undermines our values of liberty and justice for all.

Dr. Wisdom Zerit Teklay, a distinguished global leader, community activist, and candidate for the U.S. Presidency, is a paragon of American exceptionalism. However, the arbitrary circumstances of his birthplace unjustly bar him from leading our nation. This is not only a personal injustice to Dr. Teklay; it is a betrayal of our core principles.

The natural-born citizen requirement, rooted in outdated fears, lacks foundation and is detrimental. It overlooks the contributions of many naturalized citizens who have pledged allegiance to the United States. Dr. Teklay, a naturalized citizen, embodies true patriotism. His actions, character, and dedication to American principles—not his birthplace—demonstrate his commitment.

This requirement opposes inclusivity and limits potential leadership. It denies qualified individuals the opportunity to serve their country based solely on birthplace, blatantly violating the principle of equal opportunity.

The time is now for the United States to join other nations in abolishing the natural-born citizen requirement. This change will allow all qualified Americans, irrespective of birthplace, to aspire to the highest office. We urge you to join us in calling for a constitutional amendment to remove this requirement. This crucial step would enable Dr. Teklay to serve his country and foster a more equitable democracy, embracing the talents and aspirations of all its citizens.

Join us in shaping a brighter American future, where leadership is based on merit, character, and commitment to the ideals that unite us as a nation. Sign the petition below and stand with Dr. Wisdom Zerit Teklay in the quest for constitutional equality and a more inclusive American democracy. Together, let's empower America's finest to lead!

Sincerely,

Concerned Citizens for Constitutional Equality

EPILOGUE

In the epilogue of "Dr. Wisdom for President: Beyond Wisdom - Leading with Wisdom Beyond Politics," Dr. Wisdom Zerit Teklay reflects on his journey and vision. He reiterates his commitment to promoting peace, justice, and equality, underlining the philosophy of Zerit-Tonianism. His dedication to natural medicine and peace education is evident, showcasing his belief in holistic well-being. The conclusion highlights the transformative impact of his teachings and his unwavering belief in the power of collective action for a more peaceful and equitable world.

AFTERWORD

In the afterword of "Dr. Wisdom for President: Beyond Wisdom - Leading with Wisdom Beyond Politics," Dr. Wisdom Zerit Teklay passionately reflects on the transformative journey and profound insights unveiled within the pages of this remarkable book. With unwavering conviction, he emphasizes the utmost significance of perpetual learning and personal growth, not only for oneself but for society as a whole. Dr. Teklay's resounding message resounds with an unyielding commitment to foster a world where wisdom, peace, and holistic well-being reign supreme. His concluding thoughts serve as a resounding call to action, urging readers to embrace these timeless principles in their own lives and communities, thereby catalyzing an ongoing evolution towards a more enlightened and harmonious world.

ACKNOWLEDGEMENT

I am extremely grateful to the influential figures in my life, especially my parents, Tiebe Mebrahtu and Teklay Sebhatleab. Their love and wisdom have truly been my guiding light throughout my journey. I am also indebted to my amazing group of friends, whose unwavering support has been a cornerstone in my life, providing me with strength and joy.
I would like to extend a special thank you to Dr. Michael and Dr. Monica for their invaluable guidance in helping me title this book. Additionally, I am deeply grateful to Hannah, whose unwavering belief in my work has been a driving force behind my success. I must also express my heartfelt appreciation to my siblings for their constant love and support, with a special mention to my brother F.T.S. for his diligent assistance in bringing this book to fruition.
I am especially grateful to my future wife, who has been a constant source of love and encouragement, lifting me up in times of need.
This work is dedicated to the incredible individuals who have shaped my life, including my parents, family, friends, and supporters. I also pay tribute to Eritrean and American freedom fighters, as well as global freedom fighters and abolitionists like Kwame Nkrumah and Nelson Mandela. Furthermore, I draw inspiration from the vision of the United Nations, the 1997 Constitution of Eritrea, and Dr. Wisdom Zerit Teklay's vision for Africa. May this dedication serve as a powerful tribute to

freedom fighters everywhere, inspiring future generations towards a world of liberty and unity.

ABOUT THE AUTHOR

Dr. Wisdom Zerit Teklay

A Voice Reshaping Our Worldview

Dr. Wisdom Zerit Teklay is an exceptional polymath of Eritrean-American Polymath. Renowned for his multifaceted expertise, Dr. Teklay has established himself as a distinguished philosopher, an accomplished author, an influential politician, and a renowned natural medicine nutritionist. His illustrious career is further highlighted by his role as the visionary founder of the remarkable Amazoxa Peace University.
 Embracing the philosophy of being a 'jack of all trades, master of none,' Dr. Teklay embodies a wide spectrum of knowledge and skills across various disciplines. His unique approach to life and learning has enabled him to make significant contributions in each of his chosen fields, blending wisdom with a deep understanding of the world's complexities.

Dr. Wisdom Zerit Teklay, an Eritrean-American polymath, philosopher, and founder of Amazoxa Peace University, is a beacon of influential change. His philosophy, Zerit-Tonianism, advocates for social transformation, emphasizing peace and natural medicine. A lifelong natural healer, Dr. Teklay's journey exemplifies the harmonious convergence of intellectual brilliance and commitment to human well-being. His holistic approach to wellness reflects his belief in the interconnectedness of mind, body, and spirit. As a visionary educator, he is passionate about empowering individuals and fostering global harmony. His academic distinction stems from his groundbreaking philosophy, elevating human understanding and emphasizing the intrinsic value of knowledge. Dr. Teklay's work and vision embody the principles of Zerit-Tonianism, showcasing his dedication to healing, education, and the pursuit of wisdom.

Dr. Wisdom Zerit
Teklay is an exceptional polymath of Eritrean-American Polymath . Renowned for his
multifaceted expertise, Dr. Teklay has established himself as a distinguished
philosopher, an accomplished author, an influential politician, and a renowned
natural medicine nutritionist. His illustrious career is further highlighted by
his role as the visionary founder of the remarkable Amazoxa Peace University.

Embracing the
philosophy of being a 'jack of all trades, master of none,' Dr. Teklay embodies
a wide spectrum of knowledge and skills across various disciplines. His unique
approach to life and learning has enabled him to make significant contributions
in each of his chosen fields, blending wisdom with a deep understanding of the
world's complexities.

To experience his enlightening
perspective and profound wisdom, you may visit his YouTube channel:

https://www.youtube.com/@drwisdomforpresident

For further insight into his entrepreneurial endeavors, visit his business page at:

https://g.co/kgs/9vY3aj

https://wa.me/message/MHFABY26GTQUF1

For an enriching literary experience, explore Dr. Wisdom Zerit's authored works on Amazon:

https://www.amazon.com/author/drzerit

Petition:

https://www.change.org/AbolishTheNaturalBornRequirment

For further insight
into his entrepreneurial endeavors, visit his business page at:

https://g.co/kgs/9vY3aj

https://wa.me/message/MHFABY26GTQUF1

For an enriching literary experience, explore Dr. Wisdom Zerit's authored works on Amazon:

https://www.amazon.com/author/drzerit

Petition:

https://www.change.org/AbolishTheNaturalBornRequirment

Clerk's Office of Dr. Wisdom Zerit Teklay
President of Amazoxa Peace University
President of Wisdom People Party

Office Number: +1 (615)-970-1832

Email: zeritprrcw@gmail.com

Dr. Wisdom Zerit Teklay

Author Page:https://www.amazon.com/author/drzerit

PRAISE FOR AUTHOR

Dr. Wisdom Zerit Teklay's work exemplifies a profound commitment to global harmony and intellectual growth. His pioneering philosophy, Zerit-Tonianism, is a testament to his profound understanding of social dynamics and his dedication to promoting peace and natural healing. His holistic approach to wellness, emphasizing the unity of mind, body, and spirit, showcases his deep insight into the human condition. As an educator and leader, Dr. Teklay's influence extends beyond academia, inspiring a generation to pursue knowledge, understanding, and harmony. His work is a beacon of wisdom in a world seeking guidance and enlightenment.

- DR. MONICA

BOOKS BY THIS AUTHOR

Wisdom 101: Wise Lessons To Be Thought For World Presidents And For The People Of The World

"WISDOM 101: Wise Lessons to Be Taught for World Presidents and the People of the World, 2023" is a compelling anthology of insights and strategies for global leadership in the modern era. Authored by renowned thinker Dr. Wisdom Zerit Teklay, this book is an essential guide for current and aspiring leaders worldwide.

At its core, "WISDOM 101" delves into the intricacies of governance, diplomacy, and international relations, while also addressing the crucial role of empathy, integrity, and innovation in leadership. Dr. Teklay draws from his extensive experience in global politics, offering practical advice and thought-provoking lessons tailored for presidents and policymakers.

The book uniquely bridges the gap between high-level decision-making and the everyday lives of citizens, emphasizing the interconnectedness of global communities. It advocates for inclusive, sustainable policies that resonate with diverse populations, underlining the importance of understanding cultural nuances and ethical considerations in a rapidly evolving world.

Each chapter in "WISDOM 101" is a testament to Dr. Teklay's

vision of a harmonious global society, guided by wise, forward-thinking leaders. The book is not only a roadmap for presidents but also an enlightening read for anyone interested in the dynamics of world leadership and the collective journey towards a more just and prosperous world.

This timely publication is more than just a book; it's a call to action for a new generation of leaders, dedicated to shaping a brighter future for all.

Infinite Solutions: A Solution To Everything, One World, One Flag, One Constitution"

"Infinite Solutions: A Solution to Everything, One World, One Flag, One Constitution" is a visionary work by Zerit Teklay, advocating for a transformative global political system. This ambitious book proposes the formation of a unified world under a single flag, currency, and constitution. It aims to address and solve key issues like peace, justice, prosperity, safety, and security on a global scale. The author's ideal world envisions equal opportunities and rights for all, transcending traditional national boundaries and political structures. This book is a call for revolutionary change, proposing a universal approach to governance and societal well-being.

The Champion Of Peace: Presidents Reconciliation Meeting

"The Champion of Peace" by Dr. Zerit Teklay Sebhatleab is an inspiring and thought-provoking work that delves into the philosophy of peace, justice, equality, and good health. The book offers a unique perspective on global harmony and the role of leadership in fostering a more equitable world. Dr. Teklay, as a philosopher and the president of Amazoxa Peace University, shares his vision of a world where wisdom and education are the highest forms of success. Through his philosophy of Zerit-Tonianism, he advocates for a transformative approach to global issues, emphasizing the importance of peace over war and promoting a universal ethos of justice and equality. This book is a valuable resource for anyone interested in understanding the principles of peace and the potential for positive global change.

Solutions Infinies : Une Solution À Tout. Un Seul Monde. Un Drapeau. Une Constitution. (French Edition)

"Zerit Teklay Sebhatleab est un ouvrage inspirant et stimulant qui aborde la philosophie de la paix, de la justice, de l'égalité et de la bonne santé. Ce livre offre une perspective unique sur l'harmonie mondiale et le rôle du leadership dans la promotion d'un monde plus équitable. Le Dr Teklay, en tant que philosophe et président de l'université de la paix Amazoxa, partage sa vision d'un monde où la sagesse et l'éducation sont les formes les plus élevées de réussite. À travers sa philosophie du Zerit-Tonianisme, il prône une approche transformatrice des problèmes mondiaux, en soulignant l'importance de la paix par rapport à la guerre et en promouvant une éthique universelle de la justice et de l'égalité. Ce livre est une ressource précieuse pour tous ceux qui souhaitent comprendre les principes de la paix et le potentiel de changement positif à l'échelle mondiale.

Traduit avec www.DeepL.com/Translator (version gratuite)

Birth Certificate: Judge/Elect A Man By The Content Of His Wisdom, Not By The Content Of His Birth Certificate.

BIRTH CERTIFICATE " is a profound manifesto by Dr. Wisdom Zerit Teklay and the Wisdom People Party, marking a significant shift in American political ideology. The book passionately advocates for the abolition of the U.S. Presidency's natural-born citizen requirement, likening this transformative movement to the abolition of slavery. Dr. Teklay's vision for an inclusive future where leadership is determined by capability and vision, not birthplace, resonates throughout the book. It's a celebration of diversity and equality, reflecting on the need for a more representative democracy. This book not only symbolizes a new era in leadership but also serves as a call to action for constitutional equality and a more inclusive America, urging the nation to empower its finest leaders irrespective of their origin.

"Dr. Wisdom for President: Beyond Wisdom - Leading with Wisdom Beyond Politics" is a compelling narrative by Dr. Wisdom Zerit Teklay, blending philosophy, leadership, and social change. The book advocates for a paradigm shift in governance, emphasizing wisdom and ethical foresight over conventional political approaches. Dr. Teklay challenges existing political norms, calling for leaders and citizens to create a more integrity-driven political environment. The work serves as a roadmap for developing a society where wisdom informs politics, and leaders prioritize genuine well-being. The conclusion highlights Dr. Teklay's vision of a unified world, transcending national boundaries for collective problem-solving and emphasizing global unity and cooperation for sustainable progress.

Made in the USA
Middletown, DE
04 February 2024